YOUR Sleep WILL BE SWEET

200 NIGHTTIME DEVOTIONS FOR A TEEN GIRL'S HEART

RAE SIMONS

YOUR Sleep WILL BE SWEET

200 NIGHTTIME DEVOTIONS FOR A
TEEN GIRL'S HEART

BARBOUR BOOKS
An Imprint of Barbour Publishing, Inc.

© 2020 by Barbour Publishing, Inc.

Print ISBN 978-1-64352-234-0

Scripture quotations marked KJV are taken from the King James Version of the Bible.

Scripture quotations marked NIV are taken from the HOLY BIBLE, NEW INTERNATIONAL VERSION®. NIV®. Copyright © 1973, 1978, 1984, 2011 by Biblica, Inc.™ Used by permission. All rights reserved worldwide.

Scripture quotations marked GW are taken from GOD'S WORD®, © 1995 God's Word to the Nations. Used by permission of Baker Publishing Group.

Scripture quotations marked HCSB are taken from the Holman Christian Standard Bible ® Copyright © 1999, 2000, 2002, 2003, 2009 by Holman Bible Publishers. Used with permission by Holman Bible Publishers, Nashville, Tennessee. All rights reserved.

Scripture quotations marked NASB are taken from the New American Standard Bible®, © 1960, 1962, 1963, 1968, 1971, 1972, 1973, 1975, 1977, 1995 by The Lockman Foundation. Used by permission.

Scripture quotations marked NLT are taken from the *Holy Bible*. New Living Translation copyright© 1996, 2004, 2015 by Tyndale House Foundation. Used by permission of Tyndale House Publishers, Inc. Carol Stream, Illinois 60188. All rights reserved.

Scripture quotations marked MSG are from *THE MESSAGE*. Copyright © by Eugene H. Peterson 1993, 1994, 1995, 1996, 2000, 2001, 2002. Used by permission of NavPress Publishing Group.

Scripture quotations marked WEB are from the World English Bible.

Published by Barbour Books, an imprint of Barbour Publishing, Inc., 1810 Barbour Drive, Uhrichsville, Ohio 44683, www.barbourbooks.com

Our mission is to inspire the world with the life-changing message of the Bible.

Member of the
Evangelical Christian
Publishers Association

Printed in China.

When you lie down,
you will not be afraid;
when you lie down,
your sleep will be sweet.

PROVERBS 3:24 NIV

INTRODUCTION

Nighttime is a wonderful opportunity to connect with God. Even on our busiest days, we usually have at least a few minutes before bedtime that we can use to talk to Him. The devotions in this book are written to help you do that. They give you a Bible verse or two and offer some thoughts about God's Word, and then they offer a "prayer starter"—a sentence or two to help you launch into a conversation with God.

The book is divided into the following six categories:

- Your body
- Your mind
- Your emotions
- Your soul
- Your friends and family
- Your words and actions

Feel free to jump around in the book—you don't have to go through the readings from beginning to end.

Take just a few minutes each night to spend with God, and then carry Him with you as you fall asleep. When you do, you'll notice a sweeter, more peaceful sleep. Little by little, you'll grow closer to God too.

Your Body

THE GOD WHO CREATED THE WORLD IS CREATING YOU!

Just as you do not know the path of the wind and how bones are formed in the womb of the pregnant woman, so you do not know the activity of God who makes all things.

ECCLESIASTES 11:5 NASB

Do you ever lie awake at night thinking about all the changes going on inside your body? Hormones are flowing into your blood, turning you into an adult woman in all sorts of ways. You may feel good about some of these changes, but some of them may seem uncomfortable, even scary. Hopefully, you have someone you can talk with about your feelings, but you can also tell God how you feel. He understands. He made your body right from the very beginning, and He knows exactly what's going on inside you.

God, I want to relax into Your love and understanding. Help me be at peace with the changes taking place in my body. I know that You made me when I was a baby—before I was even born—and You are still making me. If You made the world—the wind, land, oceans, animals, plants, people, planets, stars, the entire universe—then I guess You can handle what's going on in my body. . .no problem!

GOD CARES ABOUT YOUR CLOTHES!

"Has anyone by fussing in front of the mirror ever gotten taller by so much as an inch? All this time and money wasted on fashion—do you think it makes that much difference? Instead of looking at the fashions, walk out into the fields and look at the wildflowers. They never primp or shop, but have you ever seen color and design quite like it? The ten best-dressed men and women in the country look shabby alongside them. If God gives such attention to the appearance of wildflowers. . .don't you think he'll attend to you, take pride in you, do his best for you?"
MATTHEW 6:27–30 MSG

. . . .

Are you already worrying about what you're going to wear tomorrow? Maybe you wish you had new clothes to wear. Or maybe you're afraid you won't look right in the clothes you have. Believe it or not, God understands! Trust the God who makes even the wildflowers beautiful. He'll make you more beautiful, inside and out, than any pair of jeans or shirt ever could.

. . . .

God, thank You for understanding me. It's hard to believe that You can make me beautiful, but I'll try. When I start to obsess about my clothes, help me to remember Your Word and trust You completely.

HE'S FOR YOU

The Lord is for the body.
1 Corinthians 6:13 NASB

. . . .

Do you ever get the feeling that God disapproves of bodies—especially teenage bodies? After all, you probably hear plenty of "don'ts" at church. Meanwhile, your body is so much more important to you now than it was when you were younger. It wants all sorts of things—to be noticed, to not be noticed; to touch people, to not touch people; to eat, to not eat—things you probably never thought that much about when you were a kid. All these messages coming at you from your body can make you feel happy, guilty, angry, scared, rebellious, frustrated, or confused.

But you don't have to lose sleep over these feelings! God does not disapprove of your body; He's *for* your body. Everything He wants for you includes making your body as healthy, safe, and happy as it can possibly be.

. . . .

God, thank You that You are always on my side.
When my body's messages seem overwhelming, remind
me to trust You. Guide my life in the direction that
will make me the best I can be physically.

DIFFERENT IS INTERESTING!

No one ever hated their own body, but they feed and care for their body, just as Christ does the church.
EPHESIANS 5:29 NIV

. . . .

This verse says that no one ever hated their own body, but the person who wrote this was an adult male, not a teenage girl. Almost all adolescents, both boys and girls (and many adults too!), have a hard time accepting their bodies just the way they are. Television, the internet, magazines, other people. . .all tell us we need to look a certain way. No one can measure up, though, because everyone has *something* that's at least a little bit different about their physical appearance. Maybe it's a bump on their nose or their big feet or frizzy hair. But all these little differences are what make each of us so interesting. Think how boring it would be if we all looked more or less the same!

The God who loves you doesn't want you to lie awake hating your body. Instead, He wants to help you take care of your body in every way possible. You're important to Him.

. . . .

God, when I start to think about all the things I'd like to change about my appearance, remind me how much You love me—just the way I am.

TAKE CARE OF YOU!

*The spiritual does not come first,
but the physical and then the spiritual.*
1 CORINTHIANS 15:46 GW

If you're trying to follow Jesus, you're probably making an effort to pray and read your Bible. If so, that's a good thing because doing these things will help you feel closer to God. They'll help you learn more about Him and understand Him better.

But God also wants you to take care of your body. Your body and your spirit are so closely connected that you can't really take care of one without taking care of the other. If you're hungry or tired, you'll probably have a harder time feeling close to God. You may get angry and impatient more easily, or you may feel depressed and discouraged. Of course, you should bring those feelings to God, but also pay attention to what your body needs. Sometimes when you're lying awake, praying is the best thing you can do to help you relax. But sometimes you'll sleep better if you get up and eat a healthy snack, drink a glass of water, do a few stretches—and *then* pray.

*God, remind me to take care of my body's needs
so that I can be who You want me to be.*

GOD'S FAVORITE PLACE

*Don't you yourselves know that you are God's
sanctuary and that the Spirit of God lives in you? . . .
God's sanctuary is holy, and that is what you are.*
1 CORINTHIANS 3:16–17 HCSB

Bodies are wonderful things, but they can also be real nuisances. They can keep us awake in all sorts of ways—with rumbling bellies, tense muscles, aching heads, or pounding hearts. Sometimes you might even wish you could just turn your body off so that you could fall asleep more easily.

When your body is refusing to cooperate and go to sleep—maybe even *especially* when your body won't give in to sleep—that's a good time to remember that your body is God's sanctuary. That means it's His safe place: a holy place and the special spot where He feels most at home.

So when you can't sleep, try this: Imagine that you and God are going inside your body. It looks like a beautiful building, and the two of you sit down together there and relax. You don't need to say anything. . .you can just be together inside God's favorite spot—*you!*

*God, thank You for making Your home inside my
body. Remind me that my body is Your sanctuary.*

SWEETS AND YOU

*Do you like honey? Don't eat
too much, or it will make you sick!*
PROVERBS 25:16 NLT

. . . .

Pretty much everyone likes sweets: soda, candy bars, cookies, ice cream, brownies. They all taste so wonderful, and researchers have discovered that teenagers eat more sweets than any other group of people on the planet. Scientists have found that there are reasons for this: teenage bodies respond more dramatically to sweets than adult bodies, and hormonal changes can even trigger additional cravings.

All that sugar isn't very good for your body, though. Not only can it make you unhealthy, but it can cause emotional ups and downs too. The ups can feel pretty good, but the downs can be awful. Researchers say that too much sugar can even change the way adolescent brains work, making it more difficult for them to think and make smart decisions. Sugar can also make it harder for you to relax and get a good night's sleep.

Instead of eating more sweets than you need, try smoothies made from fruit or baked goods with less sugar and more fiber. God wants you to be the best you can possibly be! He wants you to do the things that will make you truly happy and healthy.

. . . .

*God, the next time I want to binge on cookies or gulp down
a can of soda, remind me that You care what I eat and
drink. Thank You that You love me enough to care.*

EXERCISE AND ETERNITY

All athletes are disciplined in their training.
They do it to win a prize that will fade away,
but we do it for an eternal prize.
1 CORINTHIANS 9:25 NLT

. . . .

Some people seem to just naturally enjoy exercise, but for others it can take a lot of self-discipline to exercise regularly. When you're tired after a long day of classes and after-school activities, you may just want to sit down in front of the television or your computer. The last thing you want to do is go out for a run or hop on your bike.

We all know that exercise can help us stay in shape, but there are other reasons to exercise that are even more important. Exercise makes your entire body healthier. It helps you get sick less often. It even helps you think better, and it makes you happier. Those are all scientific facts.

Self-discipline isn't easy, but the "prize" you're working toward—a body that's the best it can be—is truly worth it. God wants that for you. He loves you now and for eternity. If you're a person who needs motivation to exercise, don't do it because you *should* in order to get in better shape. Do it to make yourself happier, healthier, and stronger. Do it for God.

. . . .

God, I want to please You in this life,
and I want to please You forever in eternity.

GET SOME REST!

It is useless for you to work so hard from early morning until late at night. . .for God gives rest to his loved ones.
PSALM 127:2 NLT

. . . .

Are you one of those girls who pulls all-nighters before a big exam? Or maybe your life is just busy every day with school, family responsibilities, a job, sports, after-school activities, homework, church, volunteer work, and social activities with your friends. God certainly honors hard work, and He's proud of all you're accomplishing. But God also wants you to get rest.

Scientific research has found that adolescents need between eight and ten hours of sleep *every* night. You need more sleep than an adult because your body (including your brain) is growing so quickly—and trying to catch up on your sleep with marathon sleep sessions on the weekend just doesn't work. Without the sleep your body needs, you're more likely to have accidents and make mistakes.

God wants you to be at your best every day. If you have trouble sleeping because you have so much on your mind, try writing a list at night. Go through each item and ask God to hold it in His hands through the night. You can pick it up again tomorrow morning!

. . . .

*Help me to get the rest I need, God.
I want to be the best I can be.*

YOU AND FOOD

Food is for the stomach and the stomach is for food.
1 CORINTHIANS 6:13 NASB

Dieting seems to be a big deal for a lot of teenage girls. So many posts on Facebook, Instagram, Snapchat, and WhatsApp, as well as YouTube videos, teen magazines, television shows, and commercials all tell you: "Lose weight! You have to be *thin*!" Your mind can't help but take in all those messages, and then, even if one part of you knows better, you can't help but buy into them.

God doesn't want you to deprive yourself so you'll be thinner. He also doesn't want you to turn to food instead of turning to Him when you're sad. God loves you, and He wants you to be healthy and happy.

So, if you're having a problem with food and dieting, talk to God about it. Ask Him to show you what you need to do. This is a big issue for a lot of teenage girls, and God doesn't expect you to handle it all alone. Talk to an adult you trust. God can give you the courage to deal with it head-on.

God, I am so thankful I can talk to You about anything. You always understand. Help me to do what pleases You. Thank You for loving me so much.

WHEN TO SAY NO,
WHEN TO SAY YES

The mind-set of the flesh is hostile to God because it does not submit itself to God's law, for it is unable to do so.
ROMANS 8:7 HCSB

All the things we're supposed to do to be healthy—from the most basic, such as exercising, eating right, and getting enough sleep, to the more complicated, such as dealing with issues around drugs, alcohol, and peer pressure—can seem like too much to handle sometimes. You may ask yourself, *Does God really care about all that?* Well, yes, He does. The Bible makes that pretty clear. God cares about every detail of your life; and because He created you, He knows that your body, mind, and soul are all woven together within you.

That doesn't mean you can rely on your body to do the right thing, though. Think of your body as being a little like a child you're babysitting. It's up to you—your inner, spiritual part—to make the right decisions for your body. Decisions like when to go to bed, what to eat, and all the rest. With God's help, you will be able to lead your body in the path that's best for you—the one that leads to God. When you walk that path, you can go to bed knowing your sleep will be sweet!

God, teach me how to rely on Your Spirit.
Show me when to say no and when to say yes.

BODY, MIND, AND SOUL

For though we walk in the flesh,
we don't wage war according to the flesh.
2 CORINTHIANS 10:3 WEB

· ·

It's not easy to be the person God created us to be. Often, we feel as though there's a war going on inside us, with one part of us wanting to do one thing while another part wants to do just the opposite.

This is a fight your body can't win by itself. No matter how much you want to do the right thing, your body may have other ideas. The body's urges can be very powerful. But God's Spirit is even stronger; and with God's help, your spirit can win this battle. Of course, it's not the sort of battle that happens once and then is done forever. Instead, it's a war you're going to be fighting the rest of your life.

Because God is on your side, your spirit *can* win. God can make you wise enough to see the right decisions to make and strong enough to actually make them. When you live life depending on God to fight your battles, you can relax and fall asleep without guilt and without worries.

· ·

God, thank You that You love me even when I'm weak.
You know how confused I get. Thank You for always
loving me, no matter how many times I mess up.
I'm so glad that You made my body and that You
love all of me—body, mind, and soul.

PRECIOUS

*You were bought with a price. Therefore glorify God
in your body and in your spirit, which are God's.*
1 CORINTHIANS 6:20 WEB

. . . .

Jesus died for you. Your life was worth the price of Jesus' life. That's how precious you are to God. In today's Bible verse, Paul (the man who wrote these words) makes it clear that Jesus didn't die just for our souls; He also died for our bodies. He died for our entire being. So, it makes sense that we want to glorify Him not only with our minds and souls (our thoughts, feelings, and prayers) but also with our bodies (our actions).

Glorify is a word that's often used in church, but we don't always understand exactly what it means. The Greek word Paul used when he wrote this (before the Bible was translated into English) meant "recognizing and valuing God for who He really is." Another definition was "telling others about God's light and splendor."

Knowing how to use our bodies to glorify God isn't always clear to us. But at night, as we think back over our day and anticipate the day to come, we can ask ourselves: *Will doing this thing tell others about God's light?* and *Will acting in this way show that I value God?* The answers to those questions will help us see the way God wants us to go.

. . . .

*Thank You, Jesus, that You loved me enough to
die for me. Show me how to glorify You.*

LIVING FOR ETERNITY

*As you come to him, the living Stone—rejected by humans
but chosen by God and precious to him—you also,
like living stones, are being built into a spiritual house.*
1 PETER 2:4–5 NIV

. . . .

When the Bible talks about Jesus being a stone, it means that He is the foundation of what we believe as His followers. He is something solid and permanent that can't be shaken. And He wasn't just an idea or an invisible spirit floating around. He was a flesh-and-blood human being. He understood what it was like to have a stomachache or an itch, and He knew what it was like to lie awake at night, His thoughts racing. Yet, at the same time, He was God. He was the "living Stone."

Today's verse says that you are a stone too. Your physical life—the flesh-and-blood part of you that walks around and eats and sleeps—is being built into a house where God's Spirit can dwell. You're a living, breathing stone, and because of Jesus, you can live with Him forever. You are precious to God.

. . . .

*Thank You, Jesus, for coming to earth, for living inside
a body here with us. I'm so sorry that people rejected
You, but I'm so glad You understand what it's like to
be a teenager (because You were one). Help me
to be a living stone, someone You can use to
build into a house that will last for eternity.*

TRUE FREEDOM

"I have the right to do anything," you say—but not everything is beneficial. "I have the right to do anything"—but I will not be mastered by anything.

1 CORINTHIANS 6:12 NIV

Following Jesus can seem like it's all about following a bunch of rules—things that as Christians we're not supposed to do. Paul, the man who wrote today's verse, wanted us to look at this differently, though. It's not about rules, he's saying. We *could* do anything and everything. After all, Jesus came to set us free from all the rules. But not everything we can do is good for us, or it might not be good for someone else. Our actions could be harmful to our bodies, or they might even hurt another person.

When Paul said he wouldn't be "mastered by anything," he meant that he didn't want any of his actions to become addictions. He wouldn't let any habit—whether it's eating, drinking, or something else—take control of his life. He had chosen what's most important to him: God.

Is there anything that is trying to master you? As you lie in bed tonight, take a few moments to think about your answer to this question. It doesn't have to be drugs or alcohol; it could be something that at first glance seems harmless, such as chocolate chip cookies or spending time on your favorite app. Whatever it is, God wants only what is truly best for you. He wants you to be free.

God, help me to be honest with myself. Show me if anything in my life is hurting me or someone else. Give me the courage to see clearly—and the courage to change.

ACT NORMAL!

*"If you 'go into training' inwardly, act normal outwardly.
Shampoo and comb your hair, brush your teeth,
wash your face. God doesn't require attention-
getting devices. He won't overlook what
you are doing; he'll reward you well."*
MATTHEW 6:17–18 MSG

When we decide to follow Jesus, we may feel as though people should be able to tell just by looking at us. It's true that people should be able to see by our actions that we are living in a different way and that God's love is at work in our lives. But that doesn't mean we should *look* differently or put on some sort of holier-than-thou show.

Instead, we should continue to care for our bodies. We should wash and comb our hair, and we should wear clean clothes. God doesn't want us to obsess about the way we look, but He also wants us to practice good hygiene. He doesn't want us to practice our faith in a way that makes people uncomfortable and calls attention to ourselves rather than God.

When we follow Jesus, people don't have to be able to tell just by looking at our appearance—but God will be able to tell by looking inside us.

Okay, God, when I get up tomorrow morning, I'll take a shower and put on clean clothes. I'll brush my teeth and comb my hair. Thank You that You don't expect me to call unnecessary attention to myself!

YOU'RE GOD'S WORK OF ART

*For we are God's masterpiece. He has created us
anew in Christ Jesus, so we can do the good
things he planned for us long ago.*
EPHESIANS 2:10 NLT

. . . .

God is the Master Artist, creating wonderful things—an entire universe full of amazing, beautiful, special things. With all those countless works of art, *you* are His masterpiece. He loves the way He made you, and what's more, He's still creating you, making you into something new in Jesus. You have been in God's mind for all eternity.

So, when you lie awake worrying about what you look like and whether people will think you're pretty or any of the other doubts about yourself that can keep you awake at night, remind yourself: *I am God's masterpiece. God made me. He didn't mess up the job. He made me beautiful so that I can do all the things He has planned for me to do in life.*

. . . .

*Dear God, it's hard to believe that I'm Your masterpiece,
but thank You for making me. Thank You that You're still
making me, turning me into the person You had in mind
even before I was born. I'm so glad You love me.*

YOUR WONDERFUL BODY

*I will praise You because I have been remarkably
and wonderfully made. Your works are wonderful.*
PSALM 139:14 HCSB

. . . .

Have you ever thought about how wonderful your body really is? Forget for a moment what it looks like, and just concentrate on all the things your body can do. Think about the way that muscles move bones and how the food you eat is turned into energy. Consider the mysteries of sight, hearing, taste, touch, and smell. Can you explain how the neurons in your brain carry messages, responding to the outside world, moving your body, thinking thoughts? All your organs—heart, lungs, liver, kidneys, and all the rest—work together in harmony. Meanwhile, at the microscopic level, your cells are doing their thing too, nuclei and mitochondria and cytoplasm. Our bodies do amazing things, things we can't really understand, no matter how good we are at biology.

Tonight, as you fall asleep, think about just how amazing your body truly is. Spend some time imagining all those intricate processes going on inside you. God created them all. Your body is wonderful!

. . . .

*God, thank You for making my body. When I feel down,
remind me how truly amazing my body is. I'm so glad
for all the things my body allows me to do.*

RELAX!

God is within her; she will not be toppled.
God will help her when the morning dawns.
PSALM 46:5 HCSB

. . . .

When you're lying in bed at night, worrying about the day to come, it's easy to focus on the negative. We think about all the things that could go wrong and all the ways we might mess up. Maybe you imagine yourself tripping and falling flat on your face in the hallway at school. . . or spilling all your food down your shirt at lunch. . .or burping so loudly that everyone hears. Bodies can be so embarrassing! If you think about it enough, imagining every humiliating thing that might happen, you can make yourself literally sick to your stomach. Your out-of-control thoughts might even lead to nightmares.

If negative thoughts are plaguing you, try repeating today's verse from the Psalms over and over until you fall asleep. It will help you have good dreams instead of nightmares and help you wake up refreshed, ready to face a brand-new day.

Instead of repeating the verse exactly the way it is, though, put yourself into the words. Say it like this and make it into your prayer:

. . . .

Thank You, God, that You are within me.
Because of You, I will not be defeated. You will
help me when the morning comes.

INNER BEAUTY

What matters is not your outer appearance—the styling of your hair, the jewelry you wear, the cut of your clothes—but your inner disposition. Cultivate inner beauty.
1 PETER 3:3–4 MSG

. . . .

We live in a world that tells us our appearance is much more important than anything else about us. We spend so much time trying to make ourselves beautiful with the right clothes, the right hair products, the right makeup, and the right jewelry that we often overlook the things that are truly most important.

Tonight, as you're falling asleep, think about the people you like best—the people you *really* like. What is it that you like most about these people? You probably don't actually care all that much about their appearance. Instead, you like the way they treat you, the way they act and talk, the way they make you laugh, or the way they help you feel good about yourself.

Those are the things God cares most about too—the things on the inside, the things that give you *inner* beauty. If you focus on that kind of beauty, then things like kindness and gentleness and honesty will grow inside you and spread out into the world, making everyone happier and helping them know that God loves them.

. . . .

When I start to worry too much about my appearance, God, remind me that my inner beauty is more important both to You and others.

THE FUTURE

*Strength and dignity are her clothing,
and she smiles at the future.*
PROVERBS 31:25 NASB

. . . .

When you can't sleep, do you ever find yourself worrying about how you'll cope with the future? Maybe you're thinking about going to college. Or getting a job. Or traveling. All the possibilities are exciting, but they can also be scary. When you were little, it was easy to pretend you were going to be a princess or an astronaut or a ballerina or a firefighter; anything seemed possible. But now the future is a whole lot closer. It doesn't seem likely that you're going to magically transform into a new, more sophisticated, more courageous version of yourself. It seems likely that when the future arrives, you'll still be just plain old you, walking around in the same old body, wearing the same old clothes.

But God is offering you a new wardrobe. You can put on the strength and confidence He's longing to give you. When you belong to Him, this set of clothing is yours for the taking. It will never go out of style. It's exactly what you need to face the future with a smile on your face.

. . . .

*God, show me what it means to clothe myself in Your
strength and dignity. Help me to understand.*

MISS POPULARITY

Charm is deceptive, and beauty does not last;
but a woman who fears the LORD will be greatly praised.
PROVERBS 31:30 NLT

. . . .

We all know girls who are pretty and popular—and yet some of them aren't nice to other people. They may be fun to hang out with, but they aren't the sort of people you'd go to if you had a problem. You wouldn't trust them with a secret. But. . .do you ever find yourself wishing you could be more like these girls? Life seems so much easier for them—at least when you're looking at them from the outside.

The truth is, though, that the things that make you popular in high school aren't always the things that will help make you successful in life as an adult. Being able to work hard, cooperate with others, and treat each person you meet with kindness are skills that you'll never outgrow.

Most important, the woman who honors God, who stands in awe of His wonder and love, will have the sort of beauty that lasts forever. Even when she's ninety-eight, she'll still be beautiful!

. . . .

God, remind me to think more and more about You,
so that You become the most important thing in
my life. Make me beautiful with Your Spirit.

YOU'RE BEAUTIFUL!

You are altogether beautiful,
my darling; there is no flaw in you.
SONG OF SONGS 4:7 NIV

. . . .

When you look in the mirror before you go to sleep, what do you see? What image of yourself do you carry to bed with you? Is it the pimple on your nose that reappears again and again in your mind or the way your hair looks after the worst bad-hair day in history?

Banish those images from your mind! When God looks at you, this is what He sees: complete and flawless beauty. He looks at you and says, "You are completely beautiful, sweetheart. Everything about you is absolutely perfect."

Does this seem too good to be true? Remember, God would never tell little untruths to make you feel better about yourself. And He's not your mom, who's probably just a little bit prejudiced in your favor. No, God sees what's truly *real*. He sees what's eternal and lasting, no matter how big that zit is or how frizzy your hair might be. He looks at you and sees the real you—and *you are beautiful!*

Take His word for it.

. . . .

God, help me to care more about Your opinion of me
than I do anyone else's. Teach me to see myself with
Your eyes. Thank You for loving me so much.

WHEN YOU'RE SICK

My flesh and my heart may fail, but God is the strength of my heart and my portion forever.

PSALM 73:26 NASB

. . . .

We all have times when our bodies let us down. Maybe you've spent months looking forward to attending a concert, but when the night finally arrives, you come down with a nasty stomach bug. Instead of clapping and singing along with your favorite band, you're hugging the toilet all night. Or maybe you've been studying for a week for an important exam, and you're confident that you'll nail it; but then on the day of the test, you have a headache so bad you can barely think.

Why do things like this happen? Why couldn't God arrange things so that we never got sick and our bodies were always doing exactly what we wanted them to do? Well, maybe it's because of sin being in the world, making everything crooked and off-kilter. But maybe it's also because getting sick reminds us that our bodies have limits. They are wonderful creations of God, but they can only take us so far. We can't rely on them for our happiness and success in life.

Getting sick can be disappointing and frustrating. But even when our bodies let us down, God never does. His strength is always there, unchanged. You can rely on Him to get you through.

. . . .

God, thank You for being with me when I'm sick. Help me to use this time to draw closer to You. Teach me now, while I'm feeling so weak and awful, to rely on You, and then help me continue to carry that with me when my body's back to normal.

FEELING SICK

Lord, all my desire is before You; and my sighing is not
hidden from You. My heart throbs, my strength fails me;
and the light of my eyes, even that has gone from me.
PSALM 38:9-10 NASB

Do you believe that God cares when you have a cold? Or
that He hates to see you suffer with period cramps? Do
you think He feels bad when your eyes are streaming with
allergies? Or do you think He has bigger things to worry
about? Or maybe you think that if He did care, He'd do
something about it instead of letting you suffer.

It's hard to understand why there's pain in the world.
People have been trying to figure that out for thousands
of years. Sometimes we get mad at God and blame Him.
If He loves us so much, why does He allow bad things to
happen? Not just little bad things, like colds and headaches
and allergies, but the big things too, like wars and famines
and disasters. We may never totally understand—not in
this life anyway.

But the person who wrote today's Bible verse was
certain that God cares. He knew he could go to God and
complain about how sick he was feeling. He was confident
that God feels our pain. God is right there with us, hurting
with us, crying with us. He knows all about it—and there's
no pain too little for His compassion.

God, I don't feel good. My body aches. I feel whiny
and miserable. Thank You for understanding.
Thank You for loving me no matter what.

BROKEN BONES

I am poured out like water, and all my bones are out of joint. My heart has turned to wax; it has melted within me.
PSALM 22:14 NIV

. . . .

Have you ever broken a bone? Or had a serious illness? Maybe you were in a car accident. Serious injuries and illnesses can be scary. They can overwhelm our emotions and thoughts so that we can't think about anything else. We might not even feel like ourselves. It can be as if the pain has melted us into a puddle.

It's pretty hard to feel spiritual at times like this. We may feel as though there's nothing left inside of us that we can offer to others, let alone to God. Pain has eaten us up until we feel empty of everything else.

Even then, in moments when the pain and fear are so bad that we can barely escape into sleep, God is there with us. He never leaves us. He's holding us in the midst of the pain.

. . . .

God, I don't want to be sick. I don't want to be in bed, missing out on life. I don't want to hurt anymore. I feel as though my life is on hold. If I'm honest, I guess I'm angry at You for letting this happen. Thank You that You love me anyway. Thank You that I can tell You anything—even that I'm upset with You!

HEALING

Have compassion on me, LORD, for I am weak.
Heal me, LORD, for my bones are in agony.
PSALM 6:2 NLT

. . . .

God has the power to heal our broken, sick bodies. He uses doctors and nurses and medicine to bring healing to us, and He uses our own bodies' amazing abilities to fight off disease and heal broken bones and flesh. Sometimes He even works miracles, bringing healing when humans thought it was simply impossible.

When we're sick, God wants us to come to Him in prayer, asking for His healing touch on our bodies. He's longing to do everything He can to make us well again.

But sometimes healing doesn't come as fast as we wish it would. Sometimes it doesn't seem to come at all. Some people must live with a chronic condition that never goes away. And one day every one of us will die.

So, what's the point of praying when there are no guarantees that we'll get better right away? Well, the point of praying isn't that it changes God's mind. It doesn't persuade Him to do something He didn't want to do all along. Instead, it changes *us*. It helps us see things differently. It brings us peace because we'll know we've put things into God's hands. It helps us trust Him more, knowing that His love for us reaches beyond this life into eternity.

. . . .

God, please heal me and make me strong again.
I'm putting my body into Your hands.

WHEN YOU'RE TIRED

"Are you tired? Worn out? . . . Come to me. Get away with
me and you'll recover your life. I'll show you how to take
a real rest. Walk with me and work with me—watch how
I do it. Learn the unforced rhythms of grace. I won't lay
anything heavy or ill-fitting on you. Keep company
with me and you'll learn to live freely and lightly."
MATTHEW 11:28–30 MSG

. . . .

The older you get, the more responsibilities you have—more
homework, more tests to study for, more sports competi-
tions, more tryouts for plays and musical productions, and
more opportunities to work and earn money. Much of it
is fun, and it's wonderful having more independence and
getting to shape your own life. But it also can be exhausting.

God understands. He wants you to bring your tiredness
to Him so that He can help you. He wants to teach you
how to live with greater strength, relying on Him instead
of yourself. And He also understands that sometimes you
just need to stop everything for a little while. Yes, you need
your sleep; but on top of that, you need to make time every
now and then to go somewhere by yourself, somewhere
quiet where you can be alone with God. When you do, God
will refresh you—body, mind, and soul. You'll go back to
your busy life with more energy, and life will be fun again.

. . . .

God, I'm so tired. Remind me to find a time when we can be
alone together. As I fall asleep tonight, may I rest in You.

ORDINARY LIFE

So here's what I want you to do, God helping you:
Take your everyday, ordinary life—your sleeping,
eating, going-to-work, and walking-around life—
and place it before God as an offering.

ROMANS 12:1 MSG

. . . .

God cares about your physical life. There's not one piece of your life that's too little or too ordinary for Him to be interested in it. He longs for you to include Him in the whole thing. From the time you get up in the morning and stagger into the shower, when you're at school, while you're laughing with your friends at your locker or sitting bored in your least favorite class, all the way through the day to the moment you fall into bed, He wants you to include Him. He longs for you to give every detail to Him.

Why? Well, it's not because He's mean and greedy or because He wants to hang over your shoulder and keep you from having any fun. He wants to be included in your life so He can bless you, so He can protect and guide you and lead you to the things that will give you joy. He wants to make your life amazing.

You were made by God—and you were made *for* God. That means that your life is best when you give your life back to Him. He understands everything about you, including your physical life. He wants you to give it all to Him so that He can give it back to you even better than it was before.

. . . .

God, I don't understand You. I don't understand Your love.
But I want to get to know You better, so I'm giving You
my sleep tonight. Be with me even in my dreams.

BEFORE YOU WERE BORN

"Before I formed you in the womb I knew you,
before you were born I set you apart."
JEREMIAH 1:5 NIV

Our bodies give us pleasure. They also can make us miserable. There's always so much going on inside them, where we can't see. We're not aware of all the complicated interactions that are constantly going on between the hormones and neurotransmitters, antibodies and bacteria, cells and organs. It's as if there are entire battles being constantly waged inside us that we know very little about.

But God knows our bodies inside and out. He knew us when we were being formed inside our mothers. He knew us even before that, and He loved us. Each of us is special to Him. None of us is like any other; each and every one of us is beloved. And He has a plan for every one of us.

Before your body even existed, He had set it aside for you as something special, something meant just for you.

God, I'm glad You understand what's going
on inside my body even when I don't.
Thank You for making me. Thank You for loving me.
Thank You for having a plan for my life.

A LENS FOR GOD'S LIGHT

Do not let any part of your body become an instrument
of evil to serve sin. Instead, give yourselves completely
to God, for you were dead, but now you have new life.
So use your whole body as an instrument to
do what is right for the glory of God.

ROMANS 6:13 NLT

. . . .

Since God loves us so much, including our bodies, and since He was the One who made our bodies in the first place, it makes sense that He wants us to use our bodies in ways that give Him glory. The word *glory* is like the word *glorify*—it has to do with the light and splendor of God. In other words, God wants to shine His light through us. He wants our bodies to be like lenses that catch His light and then pass it on to everyone around us.

Our bodies have all sorts of remarkable abilities. They can paint pictures, build houses, and create fabrics, paper, metal, and plastic. They can soothe others who are in pain, and they can express love. But they can also hit and hurt and kill. They can consume substances that are bad for them. They can choose behaviors that put them at risk for disease.

It's up to you. You can choose to use your body in ways that hurt others and yourself. Or you can choose to give your body to God so that He can shine through it.

. . . .

God, I know that my life comes from You. In You,
I am truly alive. Help me to give my body completely
to You. Make me Your lens so that Your light will
pass through me and out into the world.

YOUR BODYGUARD

He's your bodyguard, shielding every bone.
PSALM 34:20 MSG

. . . .

The world can be a scary place. The news is full of terrible stories about shootings and disasters and crime. When we think about all the things happening in the world, even the most ordinary activities can seem dangerous.

Wouldn't it be nice to have a bodyguard? Someone big and strong watching over you every minute of the day? Someone who could see danger coming and sweep you to safety? Well, that's who God is—your bodyguard.

The world is still full of danger, of course. Odds are good that at one time or another you'll have to face something scary in your life. But even then, God is with you. Knowing that, you can look at things differently. You can be confident you are still safe in God—no matter what happens. Your life is hidden within His love. He will never abandon you. You will never have to face danger alone.

. . . .

When I'm afraid, God, remind me that You're there with me. Thank You for being my bodyguard. No matter what happens, help me trust You.

THE RIGHT TIME FOR EVERYTHING

There is a time for everything, and a season
for every activity under the heavens:
a time to be born and a time to die.
ECCLESIASTES 3:1–2 NIV

. . . .

Sooner or later, all bodies die. In a sense, death is the price we pay for being born. We don't like to think about death, though. It scares us.

But just for a moment, pretend you're a baby inside your mother. Now imagine if someone could tell you that you must leave that safe, warm place, the only place you've ever known. "Don't worry," he says. "The world out here is full of light and sound and color. It's even better than where you are now." But you have no way to picture that bigger world. And how do you even know if he's telling you the truth? Maybe when you leave your small world, there will be only nothingness waiting for you. You're terrified of birth. But all the while, you're growing bigger. Even though you don't know it, your body is getting ready for a new and bigger life.

Death and birth aren't so different, as it turns out. Right now, God is getting you ready for a wider, brighter life—a life that never ends. Whenever your time comes to pass out of this world, He'll be there waiting for you, birthing you into eternity.

. . . .

God, I hope death is a long way away from me.
I don't feel ready to leave this world. But I know You
won't ever fail me, even when I die. I can trust You.

Your Mind

YOUR AMAZING MIND

Let the word of Christ dwell in you richly in all wisdom.
COLOSSIANS 3:16 KJV

. . . .

God gave you a wonderful brain. Your brain is an amazing, mysterious thing with astounding abilities. It is a gift from God, one that gives you the ability to imagine, plan, make decisions, learn new things, remember the past, anticipate the future, make connections between ideas, and come up with brand-new ideas of your own.

Sometimes, though, especially at night when we can't sleep, it would be nice if our brains came with OFF switches. Our thoughts can run away from us, galloping along in all directions, making us excited, sad, scared, angry—all while lying still and alone in our beds.

There's a term that we hear a lot lately—*practicing mindfulness*. It's a little odd at first glance because where else can we be but in our minds? But the term actually has to do with setting aside our racing thoughts and simply resting in the present moment, this tiny space of *now*, without the distractions of memories or worries.

This is also the place where God meets us. We let go of all our own words—and Jesus, the Word of God, dwells in our minds, filling them with the richness of His wisdom.

. . . .

Jesus, when my thoughts race and I can't relax,
remind me to seek You—here, in the present moment.
Come dwell in my mind. Fill me with Your wisdom.

THOUGHTS LIKE BIRDS

*You'll do best by filling your minds and meditating on
things true, noble, reputable, authentic, compelling,
gracious—the best, not the worst; the beautiful,
not the ugly; things to praise, not things to curse.*

PHILIPPIANS 4:8 MSG

. . . .

Sometimes it seems as if we have no control over our thoughts. Fears overcome us, distracting us from everything else. Or we lie awake worrying about something. We find ourselves remembering again and again the mean thing our friend said to us. We think about how mean a teacher was or how unfair our parents were or how just plain awful our siblings are. These thoughts fill our minds, pushing out prayer and love and joy. But what can we do about it?

We have the power to choose what we think. There's a saying: "You can't keep birds from flying over your head, but you can keep them from building a nest in your hair." In other words, we can't keep negative thoughts from flitting through our minds, but we *can* keep them from staying there. We can refuse to let ugly, unhappy thoughts build a nest in our minds. And we can ask God to fill our minds with His thoughts of love, joy, and hope.

. . . .

*God, help me with my thoughts. Remind me to avoid
thoughts that pull me away from You.*

GOD'S THOUGHTS

So I tell you and encourage you in the Lord's name not to live any longer like other people in the world. Their minds are set on worthless things.

EPHESIANS 4:17 GW

. . . .

Allowing God to fill your mind with His thoughts isn't easy. One of the things that makes it especially hard is that you're constantly bombarded by other people's thoughts. You turn on the television, and your head fills up with the ideas portrayed in the show you're watching. You look at the internet, and you absorb a stream of thoughts from your "friends" online. You go to school, where you're surrounded by conversations that are often mean and ugly. Everywhere you turn, it seems as though all people think about is money, appearance, and drawing attention to themselves. When people's thoughts focus on things like that, it shapes the way they live. They're more likely to be selfish; they're less likely to be kind to others or put the needs of others ahead of their own.

God wants us to live a different sort of life. But for that to happen, we must stop absorbing the thoughts of everyone and everything around us. That's probably going to mean that we will need to spend less time sitting in front of a screen and more time praying and reading the Bible. We need to make space in our minds for God's thoughts.

. . . .

*God, fill me with Your thoughts.
Show me how to focus on You.*

YOU'RE NOT A KID ANYMORE

Let the wise listen and add to their learning,
and let the discerning get guidance.
PROVERBS 1:5 NIV

You've reached the stage of life where it's time for you to make up your own mind about a lot of things. You're no longer a child. In just a few more years, you'll be an adult. It's time for you to stop relying completely on the adults in your life and to start thinking more for yourself. Somehow, though, it seems like the adults around you don't always realize that you're not a kid anymore. It can make you feel angry, frustrated, and rebellious. Sometimes you can't wait to be an adult, when no one can tell you what to do.

Actually, that's never going to happen! Adults still must follow rules. They must listen to people in authority, whether that's their bosses at work or government officials. They also have to ask for advice when they need it—and then accept it.

Part of being an adult is learning to listen to others. Everyone has had different experiences, and they've learned different things. Odds are good that people who have lived longer have learned more. We can benefit from their wisdom. We can listen and learn from them.

God, thank You that You don't think I'm just a kid.
Help me not to always feel as though I must
prove something to the grown-ups around me.
Give me the maturity to listen and learn.

MAKE UP YOUR OWN MIND

Then we will no longer be little children, tossed and carried about by all kinds of teachings that change like the wind. We will no longer be influenced by people who use cunning and clever strategies to lead us astray.

EPHESIANS 4:14 GW

The world is full of ideas. That's always been the case, but before the internet, those ideas could take years to travel around the globe. Today, though, an idea that starts in Australia can be in Idaho by the next morning and in Paris by noon. Ideas spread like wildfire.

That can be a good thing, but it can also be a bad thing if we find ourselves chasing after every new idea that comes along. One day we're all about the latest fad in fashion, the next day we're obsessed with the series finale of our favorite television show, and the day after that we're thinking about a celebrity romance. All those ideas can be interesting and exciting, but it can be hard to stay on track with God if our minds are running in so many directions. It's okay to enjoy the internet and television, but we need to be careful that we're not also absorbing ideas that lead us away from God.

God, give me strength and courage and determination to think for myself—and choose Your way.

YOUR IMAGINATION

*Casting down imaginations. . .and bringing into captivity
every thought to the obedience of Christ.*
2 CORINTHIANS 10:5 KJV

The imagination can be a good thing. It's a wonderful gift from God that allows us to come up with new ideas. It's the source of all the creativity that produces stories and artwork and music and dance. It allows us to reach out toward ideas we can't really grasp or understand, ideas about God and the things He's doing in the world.

But the imagination can also torment us (especially at night, when we're trying to fall asleep). It can grab on to a little worry and run away with it until it turns into an enormous fear with an entire story line. The imagination can create scenarios that just aren't true. It can see slights and insults where none were intended or turn shadows into monsters.

Jesus doesn't want our imaginations to control our minds. He wants our minds to be filled instead with His peace and love and joy. For that to happen, sometimes we have to throw a net over our thoughts and pull them in before they can go too far. We must tell them to just *stop* and be quiet—and then listen to what Christ has to say.

*Jesus, show me how to capture my imagination
before it runs away. I don't want my fears
to control my imagination any longer.*

HEAVEN'S THOUGHTS

Think about the things of heaven,
not the things of earth.
Colossians 3:2 NLT

. . . .

When the Bible says to think about the things of heaven, what do you think it means? Are we supposed to go around thinking about streets of gold? Imagining angels playing harps on fluffy clouds? You probably know that's silly. But what *are* the things of heaven? How can we think about a place we've never seen?

In the original language of the New Testament, the word that's used here for *heaven* meant simply "a higher place, a higher level." In the verse right before this, Paul (the man who wrote this part of the Bible) told us to keep reaching for the things that are on Christ's level, that plane of thought that's higher than the world's perspectives.

This makes it easier to understand what the "things of heaven" might be, because all we have to do is look at Jesus' life to see what was important to Him. Jesus cared about love, justice, giving to and helping others. Most of all, He focused on following God. He put God's plan for His life ahead of everything else.

. . . .

Jesus, help me to follow You. Show me who You truly are so that I can think about You. Fill me with Your thoughts.

A NEW SELF

Be made new in the attitude of your minds;
and. . .put on the new self, created to be like
God in true righteousness and holiness.
EPHESIANS 4:23–24 NIV

. . . .

In Jesus, you become a new person—the person God always intended you to be. But becoming this new self isn't something you can do once and then be done with it for the rest of your life. It's a decision that you must make over and over, every day of your life.

God's Spirit will help us with this by giving us the energy, joy, and peace we need to keep going. But we must do our part too. We have to put on the new self the way we put on our clothes in the morning. Without that effort on our part, we so easily fall back into old habits. Our minds are constantly being exposed to other perspectives than God's. We soak up negative attitudes, and our selfish tendencies rear up and take over. That's why our minds need to be constantly renewed—in other words, made new again and again and again.

We were created to be like God. That's a pretty amazing statement! But God never takes away our ability to decide who we want to be. He never turns us into robots who serve Him automatically. We get to choose. Do we want to be the old, selfish, sad versions of ourselves—or do we want to be like God?

. . . .

Tomorrow morning, God, when I get up, remind me to
put on the new self You created me to be.

GOD'S VOICE

Don't try to figure out everything on your own. Listen for
GOD's voice in everything you do, everywhere you go.
PROVERBS 3:5–6 MSG

. . . .

When you were younger, you probably relied on the grown-ups in your life to explain the world to you. You were full of questions—"Why is the sky blue?" "Is Santa Claus real?" "Where do babies come from?" "How come birds can fly and we can't?" When grown-ups gave you an answer, you probably believed them. As you've grown older, though, you've probably realized that adults don't actually know all the answers. You've begun to want to figure things out for yourself. And that's a good thing. It's an important part of growing up.

But no matter how old you get, you'll never be able to understand everything. You'll run into decisions that seem impossible to make. Things will come along in your life that simply make no sense to you. Sometimes you'll think you've finally figured out everything—and then it will all fall apart, and you'll realize you have to start over again.

The man who wrote today's Bible verse was said to be one of the wisest persons who ever lived. But he knew he couldn't depend on his own understanding. Instead, he relied on God. He stayed open to new ideas, trusting God to lead him to the truth.

. . . .

Teach me, God, to hear Your voice. I'm depending on
You to show me what's right and what's wrong.

FORGET THE PAST

*"Do not remember the past events, pay no attention
to things of old. Look, I am about to do something
new; even now it is coming. Do you not see it?
Indeed, I will make a way in the wilderness."*

ISAIAH 43:18–19 HCSB

. . . .

Do you ever doubt your ability to do something new? You
think about all the times you tried and failed, and now you
don't want to try anymore. You're sure you'll just blow it
all over again.

Our minds tend to apply past experiences to the present moment. That's how we learn. When we got burned
when we touched the hot stove, we learned not to touch it
again. When we broke the neighbor's window, we learned
not to throw a ball close to a house. But we can't apply
that principle to everything. Imagine if a toddler refused
to try walking because she'd fallen in the past. Or what if
you never learned to swim because you sank the first few
times you tried?

God doesn't want the past to hold you back. Sure, you
messed up. But now He says to you, "Forget that! Stop
thinking about it. I'm going to do something new in your
life. Look forward, not backward! I can do things that seem
as though they're impossible—and that's exactly what I'm
going to do in your life."

. . . .

*If You're not worried about my past, God, then I won't be
either. I'm ready for You to do something new in my life.*

PREPARE YOUR MIND FOR ACTION

Prepare your minds for action and exercise self-control.
Put all your hope in the gracious salvation that will come
to you when Jesus Christ is revealed to the world.
1 PETER 1:13 NLT

. . . .

We act with our bodies, but we prepare for action with our thoughts. We make up our minds ahead of time about how we want to act. If we wait for circumstances to unfold, in the heat of the moment, we may do something we later regret.

In a similar way, athletes go over their moves again and again in their heads. That way, when the situation arises in the middle of a game, their response is automatic. They don't have to stop for a minute to think about it. They're a lot less likely to make mistakes.

The same principle applies to our lives. Lying in bed at night is a good time to think about the situations that could arise in the day to come. If you know your friends like to gossip, you can practice in your head the words that will turn the conversation to kinder topics. If someone close to you is pressuring you to do something you know is wrong, you can imagine yourself saying no. When you mentally practice your responses, peer pressure and your emotions will no longer be the strongest forces in your life. Instead, you can depend on Jesus.

. . . .

Jesus, help me prepare my mind to always act
for You so that my life will reveal You to
others. I'm putting my hope in You.

SEARCH YOUR MIND

Search me, O God, and know my heart; try me and know my anxious thoughts; and see if there be any hurtful way in me, and lead me in the everlasting way.
PSALM 139:23–24 NASB

. . . .

Another good nightly practice as you lie in bed, waiting for sleep, is to go over the day that lies behind you. Ask God to help you see your life clearly.

We're so busy and life comes at us so fast that it often can be hard to see what's actually going on. We may not intend to hurt anyone, but something we said may have wounded someone deeply. Or we may think we're doing a good job following Jesus—after all, we're not getting in trouble with our parents, and our teachers like us, and we make our friends laugh—and we never notice that we've been bad-mouthing people behind their backs.

God can also help us understand our own thoughts better. He can point out to us the fear that keeps us from trusting Him. He can show us where our attitudes about ourselves and others are hurtful or unhealthy. The Holy Spirit can help us see what's really going on, but we have to make time for that to happen.

. . . .

Spirit, examine my life. Search my thoughts. Point out anything that needs to change. Lead me on Your path, the path that leads all the way through this life and into the next.

GOD'S THOUGHTS

*"My thoughts are nothing like your thoughts," says the
LORD. "And my ways are far beyond anything you could
imagine. For just as the heavens are higher than the earth,
so my ways are higher than your ways and my
thoughts higher than your thoughts."*

ISAIAH 55:8–9 NLT

. . . .

Scientists are learning more about outer space than ever
before. But even with the Hubble telescope and all the
satellites that have been sent into space, there is still so
much we don't know about the universe beyond our own
planet. We can't assume that life the way it exists on earth
exists anywhere else. The universe is a huge, enthralling
mystery that scientists will continue to study for as long
as there's life on earth.

God's thoughts are like that. If we think that God reacts
to us the way another person would, getting His feelings
hurt or getting so mad He wants to get even, then we've
got it all wrong. God's thoughts are higher than ours. We
can spend our entire lives getting to know Him, and He'll
still be too big for us to comprehend.

But this much we know: His compassion is endless. He
never gets tired or impatient. His love never fails.

. . . .

*God, I know I'll never understand You, but I want to
get to know You better. Fill my mind with Your
thoughts. Teach me to be more like You.*

FOCUSING ON GOD

Those who think they can do it on their own end up
obsessed with measuring their own moral muscle but never
get around to exercising it in real life. Those who trust
God's action in them find that God's Spirit is in them—
living and breathing God! Obsession with self in these
matters is a dead end; attention to God leads us out into
the open, into a spacious, free life. Focusing on the self
is the opposite of focusing on God. Anyone completely
absorbed in self ignores God, ends up thinking more
about self than God. That person ignores
who God is and what he is doing.
ROMANS 8:5–8 MSG

. . . .

Sometimes we feel pretty sure of ourselves. We're on a
roll, and we think we have things under control. We lie in
bed at night thinking about all the things we've done well.
We're feeling pretty good about ourselves. *Finally,* we
think, *I'm doing everything right.* We're pleased as Punch.

There's nothing wrong with feeling good about yourself. God wants you to take pride in your accomplishments.
He doesn't want you to be down on yourself. But we're
heading for trouble when we forget Him. Yet when we put
Him at the center of our thoughts, amazing things happen.

. . . .

God, I'm sorry if I've ignored You. I want Your Spirit
to live in me. Fill my thoughts with You.

DON'T BE AFRAID TO ASK

*If any of you lacks wisdom, you should ask God,
who gives generously to all without finding
fault, and it will be given to you.*

JAMES 1:5 NIV

Does it ever seem to you as though everyone knows a secret you don't? As though they've all figured out something that you still can't fathom?

We've all had that feeling. It can be a lonely sort of feeling. It makes us think that we're weird...or stupid...or immature. We think there must be something wrong with us, so we walk around pretending like we know the secret everyone else seems to know. We try to fake it. We don't want anyone to suspect that we don't actually have a clue about what's going on.

Sometimes those are the times when God can talk to us most clearly—if we let Him. When we admit we don't know something, He has room to teach us. He never criticizes us. He never thinks we're stupid. He's just glad to have the chance to teach us something new.

*God, thank You that You never judge me or get impatient
with me. Teach me the things I need to know.*

BETTER THAN GOLD

How much better to get wisdom than gold,
to get insight rather than silver!
PROVERBS 16:16 NIV

Having wisdom doesn't mean you'll necessarily get good grades. It doesn't mean you know all the facts about any given subject. Wisdom and knowledge are different.

Some people say that wisdom means you can apply your knowledge to life in useful ways. Other definitions say that wisdom is what comes from experience. It's the sort of learning you can't memorize; instead, it's an understanding that comes from life itself.

The Bible says that fearing God is the beginning of wisdom. This doesn't mean you need to be scared of God and what He might do to you. We don't need to be afraid of a God who loves us! Instead, it means we stand in awe of God's greatness and love. We realize we can't put Him into a neat little box, because He's just too big. He fills our hearts and minds with wonder. That's a feeling that puts everything into perspective. We realize what's really important and what's not. And *that* is the starting point for wisdom.

So, if you had your choice, would you choose to be rich—or wise? Your answer will prove whether or not you're already on the path to wisdom!

God, if I've tried to put You in a box, I'm sorry.
I know I can't begin to understand You. All I know
is that You love me. And that's more important
to me than all the riches in the world.

GOD'S FOOLS

Don't fool yourself. Don't think that you can be wise merely by being up-to-date with the times. Be God's fool—that's the path to true wisdom. What the world calls smart, God calls stupid.
1 CORINTHIANS 3:18–19 MSG

. . . .

We all know people who have an opinion about everything. No matter the topic, they can talk about it at length. Whether it's politics, science, technology, or the latest fashion trend, they have all the facts. They like to talk on and on, making sure everyone around them knows just how smart and informed they are. People like that can be intimidating. They can make us feel afraid to say anything for fear of exposing our own ignorance. Know-it-alls are also annoying! If we're honest, though, just maybe we can recognize a little bit of ourselves in this description.

The Bible says that people who look like they're smart may actually be pretty silly from God's perspective. With all their talk, they're only exposing the fact they're ignorant about what's most important. They're like the emperor in the story "The Emperor's New Clothes." He thought he was wearing a fancy new suit when really he was stark naked.

Meanwhile, the world often dismisses gentle, loving people. People who put the needs of others ahead of their own can look like they're being pretty stupid. But they're God's fools. They know what's important in life.

. . . .

*God, I want to be Your fool.
Show me what's truly most important.*

TIME

*Teach us to number our days carefully so that
we may develop wisdom in our hearts.*

PSALM 90:12 HCSB

. . . .

People say it all the time: "There's just not enough time
in the day." The real problem is that we're trying to fit too
many things into the day, and then we lie in bed feeling
guilty that we didn't get more done. We try to figure out
how we can fit in more tomorrow. We're so busy and our
thoughts are so full of all our activities that there's not
much space left over where God's wisdom can take root
and grow in our minds.

When the Bible tells us to number our days, it's saying
that we need to be careful with the time we've been given.
God gave us the exact amount of time we need for the
things He wants us to do. This means we can't say yes to
everything that comes along. We have to choose only what
will fit comfortably into a day, with time left over for relaxing. Most of all, we must make sure there's time for God!

. . . .

*God, thank You for the time You've given me.
Teach me to use my time wisely. Show me
when to say yes and when to say no.*

ACCEPTING INSTRUCTION

The wise are glad to be instructed,
but babbling fools fall flat on their faces.
PROVERBS 10:8 NLT

. . . .

Do you enjoy being taught? Or do you sometimes resent having to listen to adults telling you how to do things?

Most teenagers have times when they feel impatient with adults' instructions. They want to get out there and do things for themselves without anyone looking over their shoulders. They're positive they can figure it out by themselves. They may even be able to do it better than the adults!

The Bible, though, says that it's wiser to accept instruction, to be eager to learn in whatever way we can. It makes sense to learn from those who have experience, whether driving a car, baking a cake, or building a relationship. That way we can benefit from their mistakes. They can give us a head start on whatever it is we're trying to learn.

When we learn from others' instruction, it doesn't take away our independence. In fact, it makes us able to become independent that much more quickly because we don't have to waste time falling flat on our faces!

. . . .

God, help me to accept instruction with patience and
respect. I want to be willing to learn all that I can so
that I can grow into the adult You want me to be.

GOD'S WORD

For the word of God is alive and active. Sharper than any double-edged sword. . .it judges the thoughts and attitudes of the heart. . . . Everything is uncovered and laid bare before the eyes of him to whom we must give account.
HEBREWS 4:12–13 NIV

. . . .

God's Word is not something dead and inanimate; it's not just some old book with a leather cover. His Word includes all the ways in which He communicates to us—through the Bible, through Jesus' life, through the Holy Spirit in the world around us. The Word is alive, and it does things. It changes the world, and it has the power to change you. It shines through your hidden thoughts; it exposes the real motivations that lie behind your actions. It might feel as though a sword is slicing through your mind, separating what's true from what's false. You can't hide from it—and that can be uncomfortable. It can hurt.

But if you keep reading the verses in Hebrews that follow today's scripture, you'll find these words of comfort:

> *We do not have a high priest who is unable to empathize with our weaknesses, but we have one who has been tempted in every way, just as we are—yet he did not sin. Let us then approach God's throne of grace with confidence, so that we may receive mercy and find grace to help us in our time of need.* (Hebrews 4:15–16 NIV)

. . . .

Show me, Jesus, where I'm lying to myself and others. Thank You that You understand my weakness. Help me follow You.

PROVE IT

If you are wise and understand God's ways, prove it by living an honorable life, doing good works with the humility that comes from wisdom.
JAMES 3:13 NLT

. . . .

Suppose at the end of the school year, you said to your math teacher, "Yes, I've learned everything you taught me." Now imagine that he said to you, "Okay, that's good. And since you've learned everything I taught you, I'll give you an A on your report card." That's not the way it works though, is it? Instead, you usually have to prove you know and understand the material by getting a good grade on an exam.

When it comes to the wisdom of God, there are no grades and no report cards. But we still can't simply claim we understand God's ways. Words alone don't mean much. We must prove our understanding with our lives. True wisdom doesn't talk about itself. Instead, it leads to acts of kindness. It makes us humble, not self-centered or arrogant or selfish.

The closer we get to God, the more we think His thoughts—and that changes the way we live.

. . . .

God, show me how to act with wisdom. Take away my selfishness. Teach me to do Your work by showing Your love to others.

SHINE!

The Message that points to Christ on the Cross seems like
sheer silliness. . . . So where can you find someone truly
wise, truly educated, truly intelligent in this day and age?
Hasn't God exposed it all as pretentious nonsense?
Since the world in all its fancy wisdom never had a clue
when it came to knowing God, God in his wisdom took
delight in using what the world considered dumb.
1 CORINTHIANS 1:18–21 MSG

. . . .

God's wisdom doesn't look like the world's ideas about what's smart. The world says that smart people make more money. God says that love is far more important than wealth. The world says that if you're smart, you'll look after yourself first and foremost. God says the wisest person who ever lived gave His life away and let Himself be killed on the cross. The world says it's not smart to give your money and possessions away to just anyone. God says give whatever you have to whomever needs it. The world says some people aren't as important as others. God says even the smallest child is important and that absolutely everyone is loved. The world says putting God first is a dumb idea. God says that if you put Him first, He'll make you shine like the sun.

. . . .

Teach me, God, to look at things the way You see them.
Give me Your wisdom. Make me shine with Your light.

FINDING GOD ON THE INTERNET

*Watch out for people who try to dazzle you with big words
and intellectual double-talk. They want to drag you off
into endless arguments that never amount to anything.
They spread their ideas through the empty traditions of
human beings and the empty superstitions of spirit beings.
But that's not the way of Christ. Everything of God gets
expressed in him, so you can see and hear him clearly.*

COLOSSIANS 2:8–9 MSG

. . . .

Knowledge has its place, and the internet can be a wonderful place to gather knowledge. We can learn online about
history, science, nature, politics, music, and literature. We
can see into the lives of other people and have a better
understanding of how life is lived in other places. The internet can be used to spread new ideas. Without a doubt,
God lives in the internet, and He blesses us through it.

But if you start exploring every idea that's online just
for the fun of it, you can lose track of what's really important. You can also get caught up in endless arguments
online, saying mean and rude things that you probably
would never say in person.

So how do you decide how to use your time online?
The same way you decide how to live your life. Use Christ
as your standard. Look at the way Jesus lived. You'll find
everything you need in Him.

. . . .

*Jesus, when I get confused about what I should be doing
online, remind me to turn my attention to You.
Thank You that You show me God's way.*

THOUGHTS MATTER

Don't copy the behavior and customs of this world,
but let God transform you into a new person by changing
the way you think. Then you will learn to know God's will
for you, which is good and pleasing and perfect.

ROMANS 12:2 NLT

. . . .

Sometimes we think that our thoughts don't matter. After all, no one knows what we're thinking. In the privacy of our own minds, we can feel free to complain, criticize, insult, and curse. We can imagine bad things happening to the people who make us angry. So long as we don't say our thoughts out loud, so long as we don't act on them, what's the harm? Isn't this a good way to let off steam without actually hurting anyone?

The Bible says our thoughts do matter. Whether we realize it or not, our thoughts shape our actions, so if our thoughts reflect the violence we see on television or if they contain the hateful words we hear repeated by others at school and online, then those thoughts will block out God's voice. Those thoughts will make it harder for us to know what God wants for us.

God wants to transform even our thoughts. He wants to make them entirely new so that they reflect His goodness, His joy, and His perfection.

. . . .

Forgive me, God, for my thoughts when they're full of
ugliness, selfishness, and unkindness. Change my
thoughts so they're more like Yours.

SINGING WITH YOUR MIND

I should be spiritually free and expressive as I pray,
but I should also be thoughtful and mindful as I pray.
I should sing with my spirit, and sing with my mind.
1 CORINTHIANS 14:15 MSG

. . . .

Did you know that praying can be fun? It doesn't have to be something serious and boring, something done on your knees while your mind wanders. Instead, you can pray while you sing in the shower. You can pray when you're full of excitement and happiness. You can pray while you're riding the bus or sitting in the middle of study hall or cheering for your team at a big game. And you can definitely pray while you're lying in bed, ready to fall asleep. God wants you to feel free to come to Him with everything you feel. You don't need to censor your emotions. God accepts them all, and He wants you to bring them all to Him.

But God also wants you to engage your mind when you pray. He wants you to bring your ideas and thoughts to Him as well. He longs to know that your mind is focused on Him, that you're truly aware of His presence in your life. When you're thoughtful about your prayer, mindful of everything God is and wants for you, then you're less likely to get lazy and careless in your commitment to God's plan for your life.

. . . .

Tonight, God, I'm singing to You here in my mind.
I'm singing with my emotions, and I'm also singing with
my thoughts. Fill all of me with Your Spirit.

EDUCATION

Moses was educated in all the wisdom of the Egyptians and was powerful in speech and action.

ACTS 7:22 NIV

• •

Moses is one of the most important people in the Old Testament. God used him to free the Jewish people from slavery in Egypt. Moses was also the one who received the Ten Commandments from God, so you might think that God would have told Moses everything he needed to know. Moses wouldn't have needed any education from the Egyptians. After all, in the story of Moses and the Jewish people, the Egyptians were the enemy. Why would Moses need to bother with their wisdom?

But that's not the way God saw it. Instead, He used the Egyptians and their wisdom to prepare Moses for the job God had planned for him. Everything Moses learned made his speech and actions more powerful. He was able to serve God that much better.

The same is true for you. Even if your school doesn't teach you about God and the Bible, there is still plenty of wisdom to be learned from your teachers. The more you learn, the better you will be able to do the work God wants you to do now and throughout your entire life. God will bless your education.

• •

Help me, God, to learn everything I can during my time at school. Use my teachers to teach me the things I'll need to know. I want to be the person You want me to be.

STUDYING, LIVING, SHARING

*Ezra had committed himself to studying the Revelation
of GOD, to living it, and to teaching Israel
to live its truths and ways.*

EZRA 7:10 MSG

. . . .

The revelation of God is God showing us who He is. Jesus is the revelation of God. So is the Bible. God also reveals Himself to us in other ways through other people and through the natural world. Ezra, a man who lived a very long time ago, knew that he needed to respond to God's revelation with three steps.

First, Ezra studied the revelation. This means he read God's words in scripture. He thought about God. His mind absorbed everything he learned about God.

Second, Ezra lived everything he learned. He didn't *just* think about it; he also put it into practice. He let it shape his actions. He allowed it to lead his life.

Third, Ezra taught others about God. He shared everything he was learning with the people around him. He didn't do this in a fake or phony way. Because he had already made the revelation of God part of his thoughts and actions, it just naturally spilled out of him to the people he was close to. He was excited about God, and he didn't hide it.

But it all started with Ezra opening his mind to God's revelation.

. . . .

*Help me, God, to be like Ezra. Show me who You are.
I want to study You. I want to live like You.
And I want to share You.*

DECIDE FOR YOURSELF!

The people of Berea were more open-minded than those in Thessalonica, and they listened eagerly to Paul's message. They searched the Scriptures day after day to see if Paul and Silas were teaching the truth.

Acts 17:11 NLT

. . . .

How open-minded are you? Are you interested in new ideas? Or do you already have your mind made up about things?

When it comes to open-mindedness, teenagers often have an advantage over older people. Adults sometimes think they've figured things out. They may believe pretty much exactly what everyone else does in their group of friends, and the thought of questioning those ideas can be uncomfortable. When they talk with their friends, they may not ask questions or seek out new truths. Instead, they often just congratulate each other for knowing so much, while they criticize the people who don't agree with them. Teenagers, however, can be more willing to seek out the truth, even if it's scary. And that's a good thing.

This doesn't mean, though, that you should accept anything and everything that comes along. Like the people of Berea, you need to search the scriptures for the truth. Don't accept anything—even what you hear at church!—just because someone older says it's true. Read the Bible for yourself! Read entire sections, not just verses here and there that often mean something quite different when you see them in context. Let the Bible tell you what's true.

. . . .

Show me, God, what to believe.
Make Your Word clear to me.

DON'T FORGET YOUR HELMET!

*Take the helmet of salvation, and the sword
of the Spirit, which is the word of God.*
EPHESIANS 6:17 KJV

. . . .

Wearing a helmet when you ride a bike is a good safety precaution. Football and hockey players also wear helmets. If there's an accident while you're riding or playing—say you fall off your bike or run into another player going full tilt—a helmet can make all the difference between a serious injury and walking away unharmed. Not only can your brain be easily injured in an impact, but brain injury can affect your entire body. Break the bones in your hand or foot, and the rest of your body will be just fine. Injure your brain, and you may never be able to talk or walk again. You may even die. So, if your parents or coaches insist you wear a helmet, it's good advice!

The same basic idea applies to your spiritual life. Your mind is an essential part of your life with God. The ideas around you—whether at school or on the internet—can all too easily influence your mind. If you allow false ideas or destructive thoughts to injure your mind, you'll have a hard time living the life God wants for you. That's why the Bible tells us to put on the "helmet of salvation." God's Word will protect our minds!

. . . .

*I want to put on the helmet of Your Word, God.
Please show me how.*

GROWING UP

When I was a child, I spoke and thought and reasoned as a child. But when I grew up, I put away childish things.
1 CORINTHIANS 13:11 NLT

. . . .

There's a lot to be said for being a child. Life sometimes seemed simpler back then. Playing and pretending could push away sad feelings. It may have been easier to believe in God and His promises. The world might have seemed safer, less complicated, and not as scary.

But you're no longer a little kid. Now you're ready to grow up. You're ready to speak and think in grown-up ways. What will that mean to you when it comes to following Jesus? That's up to God to show you. His Word can teach you the parts of childhood to hold on to—and the parts to let go of.

And growing up never ends. Just when we think we've finally arrived, we'll realize we still have so much left to learn about God and the life He wants for us. We'll see that we're still thinking like a child. Again and again, we'll have to let go of thoughts that are keeping us from growing.

. . . .

Thank You, God, that I never have to stop learning and growing.

SPEAK UP!

"I am young in years and you are old; therefore I was shy and afraid to tell you what I think. I thought age should speak, and increased years should teach wisdom. But. . .the breath of the Almighty gives them understanding. The abundant in years may not be wise, nor may elders understand justice."

JOB 32:6–9 NASB

. . . .

Do you ever feel shy about speaking up about what you believe? Especially when you're around older kids or adults, you may feel afraid to express your thoughts. You might be intimidated by their confidence.

But the Bible says that sometimes older people have missed the truth that a younger person can see clearly. God's breath—His Spirit—breathes into younger people just as much as older people. Sure, we should listen to the voice of experience and learn from others' wisdom. But don't let that keep you from speaking up for the truth!

. . . .

God, thank You that You breathe Your thoughts into my mind. Teach me when I need to speak up for You.

GROWING UP LIKE JESUS

The Child continued to grow and become strong,
increasing in wisdom; and the grace of God was upon Him.
LUKE 2:40 NASB

The child that the Bible verse is talking about here is Jesus. Just like you, Jesus started out as a little kid. He was small and helpless in a world of grown-ups. But then His arms and legs grew longer. His body became stronger. At the same time, He was constantly learning. He learned from His parents and the world around Him, but He also learned directly from His Father in heaven. And God blessed this entire process of growing and learning. God was with Jesus through it all.

And God is with you as you grow and learn. His grace—His love and kindness—rests on you. He loves you. He *likes* you. And He's blessing you.

Jesus, thank You that You understand what it's like to be
inside a body that keeps changing and growing. Thank You
that You also understand what it's like to have a mind
that keeps expanding and questioning. I'm so glad
that You're with me as I grow. Please keep
blessing me. Help me be like You.

GOD'S BREATH

All Scripture is God-breathed and is useful for teaching,
rebuking, correcting and training in righteousness.
2 TIMOTHY 3:16 NIV

. . . .

Different versions of the Bible use different words for the same ideas. The Greek word that is often translated as *spirit* can also be translated as *breath*. We can say that God sends His Spirit out into the world, and we can also say that God sends His breath into everything, making it come to life in Him. This verse is saying the scripture is God-breath. It comes directly from God, bringing life to us.

That means that the Bible can be pretty useful to us. We can learn from it. We can trust it to shape our beliefs. It can show us where our thinking has gone off track. It can teach us to get our thoughts straight, aligned with what God wants.

The good thing about it is that you can read the Bible for yourself. A long time ago, before books were so common, not many people had Bibles of their own. Not many people could even read. This meant they had to rely on church leaders to tell them what the Bible said. But you don't have to. You can go directly to scripture. You can breathe in God's breath for yourself.

. . . .

Thank You, God, for Your Word.
Thank You for breathing Your Spirit into my life.

Your Emotions

LIFE'S ROLLER COASTER

When troubles of any kind come your way, consider it an opportunity for great joy. For you know that when your faith is tested, your endurance has a chance to grow. So let it grow, for when your endurance is fully developed, you will be perfect and complete, needing nothing.

JAMES 1:2–4 NLT

Adolescent life is full of emotions. One minute you're excited, feeling so happy you think you might be able to fly. The next minute you're so down you can't keep from crying. The minute after that, you're furious. And then you're giggling out loud. Hormones, those chemical messengers inside your body, play a big part in the way your emotions are all over the place. They make life interesting—but it can also be pretty confusing.

The adults in your life may feel frustrated with your wild emotions. Sometimes *you* may feel frustrated. But God never is. He understands exactly what's going on inside you. He's right there with you on the roller-coaster ride.

If you can learn to trust God in the midst of your teenage emotions, you'll be ready for whatever life throws at you. It's like you're in training. So long as you keep depending on God to get you through, your endurance—your ability to keep going no matter what—will keep growing. With God's help, your faith in Him will become strong.

I'm glad You understand me, God, even when no one else does, even when I don't understand myself. I'm depending on You to get me through.

CONTROL YOUR THOUGHTS

I will set no worthless thing before my eyes.
PSALM 101:3 NASB

. . . .

Our thoughts have enormous power over our emotions and actions. Thoughts can make us feel out of control and desperate. They can remind us of our faults and mistakes, making us feel inferior. They can fill us with discouragement and hopelessness. Eventually the things our thoughts focus on will also shape who we are as people. They'll play out in our lives, steering us in directions that are different from God's plans for us.

But we can choose what we want to look at with our mind's eye. It takes effort and patience. At first, we'll slip up often and fall back into old habits. But like anything else, it will get easier with practice. Practice long enough, and dwelling on positive things instead of negative will become a habit.

When you intentionally change your thoughts, your life will change too.

. . . .

God, my thought patterns have been getting in the way of my faith in You. Negative thoughts have filled me with doubt and fear and self-hatred. I want Your Spirit to blow all those tired, sad thoughts away. Breathe Your thoughts into my mind tonight.

HOT TEMPERS

Hot tempers start fights; a calm,
cool spirit keeps the peace.
PROVERBS 15:18 MSG

. . . .

God made all our emotions, including anger, so it's no sin to get angry. In fact, even Jesus got angry. Anger can give us the courage to speak up against injustice. It can help us dare to take a stand for what's right.

But anger is also dangerous. When we're angry, we often aren't thinking very clearly. Before we realize what we're doing, we can hurt someone either physically or verbally. Expressing our anger in words or action can feel good at the time, but later we'll probably regret what we said or did, because anger has the power to wound relationships. It can start fights that grow and grow until neither side really remembers what started the disagreement.

So the Bible warns us about letting our anger take control of us. We need to find positive ways to express our anger, ways that won't hurt anyone. Try writing in your journal when your temper threatens to run away with you. Talk to God about what you're feeling. Remember, you can pray anytime and anyplace. Ask God to calm your anger and turn it into peace.

. . . .

God, I ask Your forgiveness tonight for the times when
I've hurt someone with my angry words and actions.
Show me now how to make things right. Use me
to bring peace to the people around me.

DON'T WORRY!

"Can all your worries add a single moment to your life?"
MATTHEW 6:27 NLT

. . . .

Worry is one of the most bothersome emotions. It can keep us awake when we should be asleep. It can even wake us up after we've fallen asleep. Worry fills our hearts with anxiety. It can make our hearts beat fast and our stomachs ache. It's a nuisance!

Most of our emotions are useful. Fear can tell us when to run away from danger. Anger can inspire us to take action to make things right. Happiness often draws us closer to God and others. Laughter is just plain fun! But worry seldom accomplishes one single thing.

Worry and fear are different from each other. Fear comes in response to something that's going on right now—a snarling dog running toward you, a doctor's needle about to plunge into your arm, or the challenge of standing up in front of the class to give an oral report. Worry, on the other hand, is dwelling on something bad that hasn't happened. And it may never happen!

Instead of worrying at night, try praying. Replace your worries with prayers. Worries don't change anything, but prayer does.

. . . .

God, whenever I find myself worrying, remind me to pray instead. Replace my worries with Your peace.

GOD CARES

Give all your worries and cares to God,
for he cares about you.
1 PETER 5:7 NLT

· ·

Our bodies, minds, emotions, and spirits are all connected. You can't split one off from the other. What affects one will usually affect all the others. Our emotions can interfere with our spiritual lives. They can get in the way of our thinking, and they can make us physically ill. Worry can be a particularly destructive emotion.

Say you're worried about something you're afraid might happen. Your anxiety can go on for days while you wait to see what will actually take place. You can feel other emotions alongside anxiety, so during that time, you might also feel happy, angry, sad, frustrated, excited, and much more—but your anxiety is always in the background. It might mean you have trouble concentrating on your schoolwork. Worry can be especially intense at night, when there's nothing going on to distract you from it. Too much anxiety can also dull your appetite or make you eat more.

God sees what's going on—and He cares. He hates to see you so upset. He longs to give you His peace. And if you let Him, He will!

· ·

When worry eats at my mind, soul,
and body, God, show me how to give it to You.
Teach me to trust You more so I worry less.

BEST FRIENDS

"Do not let your hearts be troubled.
You believe in God; believe also in me."

JOHN 14:1 NIV

. . . .

Jesus spoke these words to His friends. He knew they believed in God, but now He wanted them to believe in Him too.

A lot of people believe in God. In 2018, the Pew Research Center did a survey to find out how many Americans think there is a God. The survey found that 90 percent of Americans say they believe God exists. Even people who said they didn't practice any religion still had some sort of belief in God.

But you can believe in God without really thinking much about Him. You can believe He exists without having an actual relationship with Him. God is a hard idea to wrap our minds around. After all, we can't see Him or touch Him. We may know He exists but find it difficult to believe He cares about whether we're happy, sad, scared, or angry. Belief in God alone won't change the way we live our lives.

But Jesus came to earth as a human being to help us go a step further in our belief. In Jesus, we see God in human form. Through Jesus, we can come to God in a new way, as friends. When troubles come along, we can take them to Jesus, knowing that He is our best friend, the One who always understands, who always cares.

. . . .

Jesus, thank You for being my best friend.
Tonight, help me to feel Your presence close to me.

WHEN YOU'RE ON THE RECEIVING END OF GOSSIP

Unfazed by rumor and gossip, heart ready,
trusting in GOD, spirit firm, unperturbed,
ever blessed, relaxed among enemies.
PSALM 112:7–8 MSG

. . . .

Have you ever found out that your friends have been talking about you behind your back? Maybe they've been saying things about you that aren't true, or maybe one of your friends has shared a secret you trusted her to never tell. Either way, it's a pretty awful feeling, the sort of feeling that can make you squirm as you lie in bed at night. You may feel angry that your friends would betray you like that, but you also may feel hurt. You may feel embarrassed and ashamed as well.

The person who wrote this verse in the Psalms understood all about those feelings. But when he took his emotions to God, he found that things changed. The rumors and gossip didn't go away, but they no longer bothered him so much. Trusting God, he could relax. He stopped feeling embarrassed. Secure in God's love, he could stand tall again.

And so can you!

. . . .

God, make me strong enough in Your love and secure
enough in my relationship with You that I can
forgive those who have hurt me so badly.

CALM IN THE STORM

Immediately, Jesus said,
"Calm down! It's me. Don't be afraid!"
MATTHEW 14:27 GW

. . . .

Jesus' friends were out on a boat in the sea when a storm arose. Their little fishing boat was tossed back and forth by the wind and the waves. As they struggled to control the boat, they looked up and saw Jesus coming toward them. But instead of feeling comforted by His presence, they were terrified. You know why? Because the person they saw approaching the boat was walking on the water!

That's when Jesus told them to calm down. "It's Me!" He shouted to them. "You don't need to be scared." And when He climbed into their boat, the storm also calmed down.

Sometimes, life can be pretty scary. Everything seems to be shifting, changing too fast for us to keep up. We feel out of control. In fact, we feel pretty terrified. It doesn't seem possible that Jesus could be with us, not when everything seems to be falling apart.

But that's exactly when Jesus wants us to listen for His voice. He's right there with us in the storm. "Don't be scared," He's saying. "I'm right here with you. It's Me, the One who loves you more than anyone."

. . . .

When my life feels out of control, Jesus, help me to hear
Your voice. Thank You that You are with me.

PEACE

"I'm telling you these things while I'm still living with you.
The Friend, the Holy Spirit whom the Father will send at my
request, will make everything plain to you. He will remind
you of all the things I have told you. I'm leaving you well
and whole. That's my parting gift to you. Peace. I don't
leave you the way you're used to being left—feeling
abandoned, bereft. So don't be upset."
JOHN 14:25–27 MSG

Has anyone ever left you? Maybe a friend moved to another town where you can no longer see her. Maybe a parent moved out of your house. Or maybe someone you loved died. When someone leaves, no matter the reason, we may feel angry and hurt. Most of all, we feel sad and lonely. Even though we know the person didn't mean to hurt us, we feel abandoned.

When the time came for Jesus to leave this earth, He knew how His friends would feel. They loved Him and depended on Him. How were they going to manage without their friend? So, Jesus gave them a goodbye gift. He sent His Spirit to stay with them, to be their friend even when they could no longer see His body. He took all their sadness and loneliness and replaced it with peace.

Jesus, when I feel lonely and abandoned, remind me that
Your Spirit will never leave me. Give me Your peace.

NEVER ALONE

This, my best friend, betrayed his best friends; his life
betrayed his word. All my life I've been charmed by his
speech, never dreaming he'd turn on me. His words,
which were music to my ears, turned to daggers in
my heart. Pile your troubles on GOD's shoulders—
he'll carry your load, he'll help you out.
PSALM 55:20–22 MSG

. . . .

Not many things hurt as much as being betrayed by someone we trusted. It feels as though we took a step, confident that we were walking on solid earth. Instead, we found there was nothing under our feet, nothing at all, and we were tumbling in free fall through thin air. It's a terrible feeling!

Jesus understands this feeling because He too was betrayed by friends. Judas, one of His followers, led Jesus' enemies to Him. Then when His enemies had taken Him away to be killed, Jesus' close friend Peter refused to even admit he knew who Jesus was.

When our hearts are aching from a friend's betrayal, we don't have to carry the pain and hurt alone. We can go to Jesus. He'll take the weight off our shoulders and carry it for us. He's always ready to help.

. . . .

Jesus, I'm so sorry that Your friends betrayed You.
I'm even sorrier for the times that I've turned away
from You. Thank You for being my friend.
Thank You for helping me carry
this pain I'm feeling.

RELAX!

So refuse to worry, and keep your body healthy.
ECCLESIASTES 11:10 NLT

. . . .

Once worries get a grip on you, you may feel as though you're helpless. But you're not! You need to call on your mind for help. Get control of your thoughts. Obsessing about all the things that can go wrong only makes your anxiety expand like a balloon that's been blown so big it's on the point of popping. Replace your worries with other thoughts. Find ways to relax both physically and mentally.

But be careful how you do this. Sometimes the things we think will help us relax can actually make things worse. Chilling out in front of a TV or computer isn't true relaxation; depending on what you're looking at, it could even make your anxiety worse. The same is true for alcohol, drugs, or tobacco. At first, they may seem to relieve your anxiety, but it's a false relaxation that doesn't last. Worry can actually harm your body—but so can alcohol, drugs, and tobacco. Using them can make your situation even worse.

Instead, try taking deep breaths. With each breath you take in, say to God (either out loud or silently inside your head), "I give this to You." Then, as you breathe out, say, "I trust You." Practicing a relaxation technique like this will help keep you healthy—body, mind, and soul.

. . . .

*Remind me, God, to turn to You whenever
I realize I'm starting to worry. Replace my
anxiety with Your peace and love.*

BUILDING ENDURANCE

*We can rejoice, too, when we run into problems and
trials, for we know that they help us develop endurance.
And endurance develops strength of character,
and character strengthens our confident hope of salvation.*
ROMANS 5:3–4 NLT

. . . .

If you're training for track or cross-country, endurance
has to do with your muscles' ability to keep going even
when they're tired. The stronger your muscles are, the
more endurance you'll have—and the more you run, the
stronger you'll grow. Emotional endurance is a similar idea.
The more experience you have with emotional upsets,
the more strength you'll have to deal with the next set of
troubles that come around. You'll be able to keep going
even when life gets hard.

In the middle of a bad day, it's tempting to throw up
our hands and scream, "I can't take this anymore!" But
expressing that feeling of frustration and helplessness can
actually make our emotions even harder to handle. Instead,
try saying to yourself, "This is a rotten situation, but with
God's help, I can handle it. I can get through it. He's using
this to make me stronger and stronger."

. . . .

*I don't like what's going on in my life, God. Honestly,
I don't feel much like rejoicing about it! But I trust You.
I know You're helping me grow strong. With You by
my side, I can handle whatever life throws at me.*

LET IT GO

*Go ahead and be angry. You do well to be angry—
but don't use your anger as fuel for revenge. And don't
stay angry. Don't go to bed angry. Don't give
the Devil that kind of foothold in your life.*
EPHESIANS 4:26–27 MSG

. . . .

When anger stays, hanging around hour after hour or even day after day, it changes. It's no longer healthy. It can turn into resentment and hatred. There's a sick sort of pleasure in nursing this feeling; we dwell on our anger, plotting all the bad things we want to happen to the person who made us mad. We grow attached to our anger, and we don't want to give it up.

There's a saying: "Resentment is like swallowing poison and then waiting for the other person to die." In other words, when you hold on to your anger, allowing it to turn into resentment, it hurts you more than anyone else. It gives evil a grip on your life. It robs you of the joy and love God wants you to experience.

So let it go! If you've blown up at someone today, send them a quick text with an apology. You'll find you sleep a lot better when you do.

. . . .

Teach me, God, to release my anger into Your hands.

LISTEN FIRST—THEN WAIT!

Everyone must be quick to hear,
slow to speak and slow to anger.
JAMES 1:19 NASB

Some days it's so easy to get mad. If you haven't had enough sleep or if you're hungry, you may find yourself losing your temper more quickly. Hormones can also influence your emotions. These are good things to notice about yourself. If you're aware that you're more likely to get angry, you can be prepared ahead of time. That way you're less likely to say or do something you regret. You won't have to lie awake at night with your face burning, remembering how awful you acted!

The Bible has some good advice when it comes to anger management. Make up your mind to keep your mouth shut and listen a little longer before you react. If you take time to hear what the other person is saying, you may realize there's no reason for you to get mad after all. Counting to ten before you speak is old advice that's been around for a long time, but it's still a good strategy on those days when it's all too easy to lose your cool. It gives you time to cool down. It allows the thinking part of you rather than the emotional part a chance to come up with better ways to respond.

Jesus, teach me ways to control my temper.
Remind me to listen first and then wait
before I say or do anything.

YOUR GOD-CASTLE

The LORD is my light and my salvation. Who is there to fear?
The LORD is my life's fortress. Who is there to be afraid
of? . . . Wait with hope for the LORD. Be strong,
and let your heart be courageous.

PSALM 27:1, 14 GW

. . . .

Do you ever wish you had your own private fortress? A castle complete with towers and a moat and a tall wall all the way around it—a place where you could go to be completely safe whenever you were afraid?

God can be that fortress. Whenever life seems like too much for you to handle, when you're scared and upset, you can run away and hide in Him. When you feel alone, when even the people who love you most don't understand or seem to turn away, you can always run to your God-castle. His presence is a place of light, a place of complete security and safety. When He surrounds your life with His love, you have nothing to fear. You can be strong and full of hope.

And that's not make-believe!

. . . .

Be my castle tonight, God, the place where I can run to be
safe. No enemy can reach me when I'm hidden in You.

WHEN LIFE FALLS APART

God is our refuge and strength, a helper who is always found in times of trouble. Therefore we will not be afraid, though the earth trembles and the mountains topple into the depths of the seas, though its waters roar and foam and the mountains quake with its turmoil.

PSALM 46:1–3 HCSB

. . . .

Sometimes life seems to just fall apart. Everything we thought we could count on starts to shake. We realize that things we took for granted aren't permanent after all. Maybe someone we love dies. Maybe a relationship we've depended on starts to crumble. A favorite place gets torn down or burns to the ground. Even our families, the bedrock of our lives, can change in ways that seem scary and uncomfortable.

As frightening as all this can be, change is a normal part of life. Nothing stays the same. The older you get, the more changes you'll have to live through. Nothing is permanent.

Except God. His love is rock solid. Nothing can shake it. He will help you survive all the changes life throws at you. He will be your safe place.

. . . .

God, when the people, places, and things I love threaten to fall apart, when everywhere I look I see things changing in ways that scare me, thank You that You never change. I can fall asleep in Your arms, knowing You will keep me safe.

CHOOSE SLEEP!

This is what the Lord Almighty, the God of Israel, says:
". . .I will refresh the weary and satisfy the faint."
At this I awoke and looked around.
My sleep had been pleasant to me.
JEREMIAH 31:23, 25–26 NIV

. . . .

Getting a good night's sleep isn't necessary only because your body needs rest. Lack of sleep is hard on your emotions too. It reduces your emotional endurance so that you don't cope as well with life's hard stuff. It makes you more likely to feel anxious and depressed. That's a scientific fact.

In fact, researchers have found a clear link between lack of sleep and teenage depression and anxiety. In a study of nearly 28,000 high school students, scientists found that each hour of lost sleep meant a 38 percent increase in the risk of feeling sad or hopeless.

So, God wants you to take sleep seriously. He uses sleep to bless you in all sorts of ways—physically, mentally, and emotionally. Get enough sleep, and you'll be happier with your life. You'll find it easier to be the person God wants you to be.

. . . .

God, I want to be all that You want me to be.
Remind me that sleep is important. Use my sleep
to make me stronger—physically, mentally,
emotionally, and spiritually.

WHEN IT'S HARD TO SLEEP

*In peace I will both lie down and sleep, for You alone,
O LORD, make me to dwell in safety.*
PSALM 4:8 NASB

Sometimes, no matter how hard we try to get enough sleep, our bodies just don't cooperate. We lie in bed hour after hour, tossing and turning, unable to turn off our thoughts. If you have that problem, here are some things you could try:

- Get some exercise during the day—but not in the evening, not close to the time when you'll be going to bed.
- Limit your caffeine intake. Try not to drink cola or coffee after the middle of the day.
- Turn off your phone, computer, and television an hour or two before you go to bed. (The light from the screens interferes with your body's sleep pattern.)
- Have a relaxing bedtime routine. Prayer and scripture reading before you go to sleep is a perfect way to unwind!

Sleep is God's gift to you. He uses it to refresh you and make you happy.

Help me to sleep tonight, God, so that I can wake up happy, ready to face tomorrow. Thank You that You will keep me safe all through the night.

BOREDOM

"I will open rivers on the bare heights and springs in the midst of the valleys; I will make the wilderness a pool of water and the dry land fountains of water."
ISAIAH 41:18 NASB

. . . .

Sometimes boredom is harder to bear than emotional ups and downs. Feeling bored is often our response when our lives feel empty. Nothing exciting is happening. Nothing is interesting. We're tired of our lives. The same old things are happening day after day. Life feels dry as dust.

But you can bring even boredom to God. He cares about *everything* you feel. And when you turn to Him, focusing on Him (especially at night before you go to bed) through prayer and reading the Bible, you may be surprised by how your life changes. God has promised to open rivers of life even in the most boring days. He'll lead you to pools of refreshing water that will restore your joy and excitement in life.

. . . .

Thank You, God, that You don't scold me when I feel bored with life. I'm glad You understand. Draw my attention to You whenever my life feels like it's turned into a deep valley of boredom that I can't escape. Refresh me with Your living water.

FEAR NOT!

*"The LORD himself goes before you and will be with you;
he will never leave you nor forsake you. Do not
be afraid; do not be discouraged."*

DEUTERONOMY 31:8 NIV

. . . .

Do you ever have the niggling feeling that God's commandments take the joy out of life? All those "thou shalt nots" telling us what we can't do? Do you sometimes feel as though God's giving you two choices: obey His rules and don't have any fun or break the rules and feel guilty?

That feeling is understandable, given how grown-ups sometimes talk about the Bible; but the reality is quite different. Everything God tells us to do will make us happier and healthier, and that means life will actually be more fun. On top of that, guess what command is given over and over and over in the Bible more than any other? No, it's not "Don't lie" or "Don't commit sexual sin." Though those *are* God's commandments, they're not repeated many times. But this one is: "Don't be afraid! Fear not!"

That's right. God wants to free you from fear so much that this command is repeated, in one form or another, at least 365 times in the Bible. That's one per day for an entire year—a reminder that God is there with you each and every day. He's with you today. He'll be with you tomorrow. You don't need to be afraid anymore.

. . . .

*Take away my fear, God. Help me to
feel Your presence with me tonight.*

YOUR HEART'S DESIRE

Trust in the LORD and do good. . . . Take delight in the LORD, and he will give you the desires of your heart.
PSALM 37:3–4 NIV

God wants you to put Him first in your life. He wants to use you to help other people, to make the world a better place. He wants you to be happy. When we put our trust in God, allowing Him to use us, our lives fill with joy. Bad things will still happen, of course. Some days we'll feel sad, and we'll still get angry sometimes. But despite all those normal ups and downs, God will send something along that delights us each and every day we spend with Him. God isn't a stingy mean old miser. He's generous and loving. He loves to give us good gifts. When we live with our hearts turned toward God, trying to please Him, He'll give us our hearts' desires.

That doesn't mean He'll necessarily give us whatever we *think* we want: that person you have a crush on might never return your feelings, you might not get a brand-new sports car for your birthday, and you might not get into the college you're hoping for. But God knows what your heart *really* wants, the things that will give you real joy, that will make you grow and become all He wants you to be—and if you let Him, He'll make sure you have them.

I trust You, God, to give me everything I need to be happy.

DON'T BE AFRAID TO ASK FOR HELP!

Look at me! Answer me, O Lord my God! Light up my eyes, or else I will die and my enemy will say, "I have overpowered him." . . . But I trust your mercy. My heart finds joy in your salvation. I will sing to the Lord because he has been good to me.
PSALM 13:3–6 GW

You're allowed to be sad. You're allowed to not have it all together. Negative emotions are a normal part of being a human being, especially when you're a teenager. God will be with you through it all, and He can bless you even on your sad days. But if you're feeling desperate, if you feel like you might die if you don't get some help, then God can use another human being to give you the help you need. Talk to someone you trust right away.

God works in many ways. Medical professionals, school counselors, teachers, and pastors are all people God can use to help you. Pray about it, and ask God to guide you to the right person. Trust Him to work through others. You don't have to go through this alone!

I'm trusting You, God, to save me from my sad feelings. Don't let depression overcome me. Bring light to my heart. Give me joy. Make me sing again.

THE LIVING ONE

This is the day that Yahweh has made. We will rejoice
and be glad in it! . . . Yahweh is God, and he has given us
light. . . . You are my God, and I will give thanks to you.
You are my God, I will exalt you. Oh give thanks to Yahweh,
for he is good, for his loving kindness endures forever.

PSALM 118:24, 27–29 WEB

. . . .

The word *Yahweh* is God's name in the Hebrew Bible. When
our English Bibles use the words *God* and *Lord*, the word in
Hebrew is usually *Yahweh*. It means the "Living One" or the
"One Who Gives Life." When God appeared to Abraham,
He told Abraham that His name was I AM. The God who
loves us is all about life. He gives life. He creates life. He
is life. And each day, He creates new life for us. Whatever
happens, He is in it, giving His life to us.

As you go to bed tonight, know that God has a new
day planned for you tomorrow, a day created by Him. He
wants you to be happy. He wants to make you glad!

. . . .

Thank You, Living One, the One who gives me life, that You
make each day. Tomorrow when I get up, remind me to
rejoice in the new day You've given me. You are so
good to me! Your kindness to me never ends.

PRAYERS INSTEAD OF WORRIES

Don't fret or worry. Instead of worrying, pray. Let petitions and praises shape your worries into prayers, letting God know your concerns. Before you know it, a sense of God's wholeness, everything coming together for good, will come and settle you down. It's wonderful what happens when Christ displaces worry at the center of your life.

PHILIPPIANS 4:6–7 MSG

God doesn't expect you to be perfect. He loves you as you are, with all your mood swings, all your flaws, all your mistakes, and all your anxiety. But He longs to make life easier for you. He wants to take away your anxiety and replace it with His peace and joy.

The cure for anxiety is not worrying less. It's praying more. When you think about it, worry and prayer aren't that different. You might say that worry is like negative prayer. Instead of saying, "Here's this situation that concerns me, God, so I'm going to trust You to take care of it," worry says, "Here's this situation that concerns me, so I'm going to imagine everything that could possibly make it worse."

You can worry or you can pray, but you can't do both. Worry takes the place that prayer would take in your heart and mind. Or prayer can take the place that worry would take. You choose.

When worries make me anxious, God, remind me to replace them with prayer. I'm trusting You to make everything work out.

CLEANED BY GOD

*"I will sprinkle clean water on you, and you will be clean;
I will cleanse you from all your impurities."*

EZEKIEL 36:25 NIV

. . . .

Do you lie awake worrying about things you've done or about things that have been done to you? Do you feel guilty and dirty? Most of us feel like that sometimes. Some of us have had experiences or have made choices that can make those feelings seem overwhelming. No matter how you twist and turn in your bed, you can't escape the yucky feelings.

But God does not look at you and see something dirty or shameful. No matter what you've done or what's happened to you, He wants you to feel clean again.

Remember, God isn't just something people talk about in church. He's *real*—and He has the power to make you feel pure and innocent. He can wash you and make you clean.

. . . .

God, You know all my secrets, all the things I don't want anyone to know. Thank You that I don't ever need to feel embarrassed with You. Thank You that You don't judge me or hate me. Please make me feel clean again.

REST AND RECOVER

I called upon the Lord in distress: the Lord answered me, and set me in a large place.

PSALM 118:5 KJV

. . . .

Stressful times are a normal part of life. They happen to everyone. With God at your side, you'll be strong enough to survive even the most painful, difficult things. But even with His presence inside you, you'll need time to recover before you go out to fight another day.

When you're doing strength training, you can't just lift weights all day long. Your muscles need a chance to recover and repair. The same is true for your heart, the emotional part of you. So, when you call to God for help, remember that you shouldn't expect Him to make you able to keep going endlessly without pausing. Instead, allow Him to set you in a "large place" where you can rest and recover.

The hour before you go to bed is a good time to enter into this space of safety and relaxation with God. Spend some time with Him, alone in your room, with your phone and computer turned off. Allow Him to restore your heart, making you strong to face tomorrow.

. . . .

Use this time that we have together, God, to make me stronger. Thank You that You're here with me.

ANGELS

I bless GOD every chance I get; my lungs expand with his praise. I live and breathe GOD; if things aren't going well, hear this and be happy. . . . GOD met me more than halfway, he freed me from my anxious fears. . . . When I was desperate, I called out, and GOD got me out of a tight spot. GOD's angel sets up a circle of protection around us while we pray.
PSALM 34:1–2, 4, 6–7 MSG

. . . .

Do you believe in guardian angels? The Bible is full of stories about angels, God's messengers, who come to help human beings. This Bible verse promises that when you pray, God's angel draws a circle of safety around you. When you feel anxious, when you are desperate with fear, just reach out to God in prayer. God is already reaching out to you. He'll send His angel to rescue you. He'll change your anxiety to happiness.

. . . .

When my heart is overrun with fear, God, thank You that You're waiting to help. I know I'll probably never see Your angels with me, but I believe they are there. When I breathe in Your presence, may I breathe out Your praise!

YOUR ANCHOR

We have this hope as an anchor for the soul, firm and secure. It enters the inner sanctuary behind the curtain.
HEBREWS 6:19 NIV

. . . .

When your emotions are all over the place, you may feel as though your relationship with God goes up and down, on and off. But that's not how God sees it. He sees past your emotions. He sees the steady part of you that's underneath all your emotional ups and downs.

An anchor keeps a ship from being washed away no matter how rough the sea may be. The ship's deck may be tilting back and forth with the waves, but because of its anchor, the ship won't capsize. God can be *your* anchor. He can see you better than you can see yourself, and He can hold you steady.

When God is your anchor, you're fastened to something far deeper than any of your emotions. Your anchor is on the other side of life's "curtain," in God's inner sanctuary in eternity, where nothing can shake it.

. . . .

Hold me steady, God.
Be my anchor tonight—and tomorrow too.

IMPATIENCE

*"For the vision is yet for the appointed time,
and it hurries toward the end, and won't prove
false. Though it takes time, wait for it;
because it will surely come. It won't delay."*

HABAKKUK 2:3 WEB

God promises you a life of joy, a life of power and love. He has plans for you. Meanwhile, you look around, and you're still the same old you living the same old life. You want to be stronger, more grown up, happier. You long to have the sort of relationship with someone that will make you feel special and loved. You yearn to do something important, something that will make a difference. You wish you were wiser, surer of yourself, more skillful. But day after day, you're just going to school and coming home, dealing with the same things. Nothing exciting seems to happen very often. You're impatient for your life to begin.

But God knows the exact right time for everything to happen. He's using this time in your life to get you ready for the future He has planned for you. Don't worry. Nothing will be late. Everything will happen right on time.

I feel so impatient tonight, God, so tired of dealing with the same things day after day. I wish tomorrow would be different from today. I feel like I'm ready for something new. Help me to trust that You know what You're doing.

THE SHADOW OF DEATH

Even though I walk through the valley of the shadow of death, I fear no evil, for You are with me; Your rod and Your staff, they comfort me.
PSALM 23:4 NASB

. . . .

When someone close to you dies, you feel sad, but you may also feel a whole bunch of other emotions. You'll probably feel scared: How could someone so important in your life disappear? How can life ever be the same? What if you die too? Where is this person now? You may feel angry—at God, at the person who died, or both. Why did God let this person die? Why did this person leave you? You may also feel numb, as though all your emotions have dried up. You may feel confused, not sure *what* you feel. All these feelings are normal. It's okay to feel all of them.

And you can take them all to God. You can tell Him that you're sad, scared, angry, or numb. He accepts it all. He understands. He loves you, and He is with you.

. . . .

God, sometimes at night I can't stop thinking about the people I've lost. My feelings are too big. I don't know what to do with them. Can I cry on Your shoulder?

ENVY

The life of the body is a heart at peace,
but envy rots the bones.
PROVERBS 14:30 WEB

Envy is one of the most destructive emotions. It not only turns you against others, but it also turns you against yourself. Envy makes you look at others and hate them for what they have while at the same time telling you that you don't have enough. You look at another girl and envy her clothes and beauty. You envy a friend's higher grades. You envy the attention that one of your siblings gets from your parents. Envy makes you want to be cruel. You want to punish others for having what you don't have. You want to spoil what they have. At the same time, though, envy makes you feel small and inadequate. You feel not good enough. In the end, envy hurts you more than anyone.

The truth is everyone lacks something. For all you know, the person you envy is envying you for some other reason. No one has everything. God wants us to use whatever He's given us, be thankful for it, and do something good with it.

So, if envy is keeping you awake at night, stop looking at the other person who seems to have it all. Rather, look at God, who has given you everything you need.

Forgive me for the envy I feel, God.
Show me how to see myself and others with Your eyes.

DOUBT

"Blessed is she who has believed that the Lord would fulfill his promises to her!"
Luke 1:45 niv

. . . .

When you think about all the promises you read in the Bible, do you ever feel full of doubt? Do they all seem too good to be true? God promises you peace, joy, love, and freedom from fear, yet you still worry and get sad. You feel lonely and scared. You wonder sometimes if the Bible is really true. You even wonder if God is real.

Doubt is not a sin. Everyone feels doubt sometimes. The Bible is full of stories about women and men who heard unbelievable things from God. Many of them doubted that God's promises would happen. They were rational, sensible people, and God's promises just didn't make sense to them. Sarah even laughed out loud when she heard what God said. God didn't punish them for their doubts. He still kept His promises to them, and He'll do the same for you.

Doubt is not the opposite of faith; you can doubt and still have faith. It's okay to bring your questions to God. Give them to Him. Don't let your doubts keep you awake at night.

. . . .

You know my doubts, God. Thank You that I don't have to pretend with You. I do believe You. Help me to believe You more.

A NIGHTLY PRACTICE

Open up before God, keep nothing back;
he'll do whatever needs to be done.
PSALM 37:5 MSG

No matter what you're feeling, you don't have to try to hide it from God. Whether you're happy, sad, angry, scared, doubting, confident, envious, or worried, share it all with God. He will never judge you. He won't think you're silly or immature. He understands.

Not only does He long for you to share your emotions with Him, He wants you to express your feelings in words. Bottling up your emotions is like shaking a soda can. Eventually you'll explode, and all those pent-up emotions will come pouring out when you least expect it. Some tiny thing at school could set you off, which could be both embarrassing to you and hurtful to those around you. It's far better to make a nightly practice of sharing all your feelings with the friend who always understands—God.

Tonight, before you sleep, tell God what you're feeling. Look back at the day behind you. Tell God what happened and share your emotions. Don't hold anything back!

God, thank You that You are the best friend anyone
could have. You always listen. You're never impatient.
You're always interested. You always love
me and understand me.

Your Soul

YOUR PRECIOUS SOUL

*"And what do you benefit if you gain the whole world
but lose your own soul? Is anything worth
more than your soul?"*

MATTHEW 16:26 NLT

Your soul is the inner part of you, the *you* that no one else can see. It's the part of you that will continue to live even when your body dies. The Bible says that your soul is the life that God breathed into you. It is the place where you and God connect most deeply.

God cares for your body. He gave you your mind and your emotions as ways for you to experience and understand life. But God loves your soul most of all. God blesses us with health and intelligence and joy, but all those things are intended for the growth of our souls—to help us become exactly what He created us to be. And sometimes He also uses illness and troubles and sorrows to help our souls grow.

God knows that your soul is more precious than anything. Being pretty, smart, and happy is all fine and good, but nothing is as important as your soul!

*God, as I fall asleep tonight, be present within my soul.
May I carry You in me all through the
night and into tomorrow.*

GROW UP!

So let us stop going over the basic teachings about Christ again and again. Let us go on instead and become mature in our understanding.

HEBREWS 6:1 NLT

. . . .

The decision to follow Jesus is an important one. Sometimes, though, we get stuck and don't move past that decision. We may even feel as though we must make the decision again and again. When we keep slipping back into old habits, we might think that our decision didn't "take." We might be afraid that we're not really Christians after all, and so we go through the whole process all over again, telling God we're sorry for our sins and inviting Jesus to come into our hearts.

We are never going to be perfect, not in this life anyway. But that doesn't mean that every time we sin we lose our relationship with Jesus. We don't have to start over from the beginning. Instead, we ask for God's forgiveness; we ask Him to help us to do better in the future, and then we move on. We focus on learning more and more about God. We spend time with Him daily so that we'll become closer and closer to Him. When we do those things, gradually we become more mature in our faith. Our souls grow.

. . . .

Jesus, I hate that I keep making mistakes.
Thank You that You always forgive me.
Help my soul become mature in You.

LOVE STORY

With both feet planted firmly on love, you'll be able to take in with all followers of Jesus the extravagant dimensions of Christ's love. Reach out and experience the breadth! Test its length! Plumb the depths! Rise to the heights! Live full lives, full in the fullness of God.
EPHESIANS 3:17–19 MSG

. . . .

Some people live their lives focusing on their bodies' sensations. Other people live mostly inside their minds, reducing life to their thoughts. And a lot of us feel as though our emotions are where our lives take place. But God wants us to live from our souls. When we do, then everything else falls into perspective.

When you go through life aware of your own soul, then you're living in a way that allows you to truly experience God's love. Every day becomes a wonderful adventure because everywhere you turn, you'll begin to see God's love at work. You'll be able to stretch and grow in all directions, knowing that you'll never reach the limit of His love. Your life will become full of God. Life's ups and downs won't matter quite as much because you'll be living the best love story ever.

. . . .

Jesus, I want to follow You with my body, mind, emotions, and most of all, my soul. Show me Your love tonight as I fall asleep. Fill me up with You.

SIN

*If anyone sins, we have a Counselor with the Father,
Jesus Christ, the righteous.*
1 John 2:1 web

In the Bible's original language, the word *sin* meant "to miss the mark." It was the same word used when an archer's arrow failed to hit the target. We want to hit God's bull's-eye as often as we can, but all of us make mistakes. The world is full of temptations that are hard to resist. When we miss the mark, there are often consequences: we hurt ourselves and others. But Jesus is still on our side. No mistake of ours could make Him stop loving us, and He can work even through our mistakes. Our mistakes teach us that we're not strong enough to follow Jesus on our own. We need His help.

So, don't lie in bed beating yourself up for the sins you committed today. Instead, take them to Jesus. With His help, you'll be able to get past the stupid things you did to impress someone. He can show you how to make amends for those mean things you said to a friend. Don't be afraid to tell Him everything. He's on your side!

*Jesus, thank You that You forgive my sins.
Give me strength to deal with the consequences
of my actions. Help me to do better tomorrow.*

SPIRITUAL FOOD

Grow in grace, and in the knowledge of
our Lord and Saviour Jesus Christ.
2 PETER 3:18 KJV

. . . .

Teen bodies grow fast. As a girl, you'll probably stop growing sooner than the boys in your class will, but even if you're not getting any taller, your body and brain are still developing. That's why a healthy diet is so important; your body can't grow properly without the right food.

The same is true of your soul. You can't grow spiritually if you aren't being spiritually fed. Growth won't happen automatically, not without food. Just as your body would become sick and weak if you were on a starvation diet, your soul will also suffer without spiritual nutrition.

Going to church isn't enough to feed your soul. You also need time alone with God every day. You need to pray and read the Bible for yourself. You need to come into God's presence, even if only for a few moments, throughout your day. When that becomes a daily habit, you'll grow in God's grace. You'll get to know Jesus better and better.

. . . .

Thank You, Jesus, for this time I have with You each night.
During these moments when we're alone together,
please feed my soul. Help me grow.

SIMPLE, EASY PRAYER

Devote yourselves to prayer,
being watchful and thankful.
COLOSSIANS 4:2 NIV

- -

Some people have marathon prayer sessions. They may spend an hour or more in prayer every day. That's wonderful, but don't feel like you have to do the same thing. Nowhere in the Bible does it specify that prayer times must be of a certain length. Instead, the Bible makes clear that prayer is meant to come as naturally to us as breathing.

If you set some huge goal for the time you spend in prayer, you may become discouraged when you don't live up to your goal. On busy mornings and late nights, when you're exhausted from a busy day, you'll probably find yourself making excuses instead of praying. Then you'll feel guilty. . .and soon you may not even want to think about praying. It's much smarter to set smaller goals you can keep. Try praying for five minutes in the morning and five minutes at some time during your day (maybe during study hall or some other quiet moment you can count on). Pray when you're in the shower or on the ride to and from school. Pray in bed as you're falling asleep.

And your prayer doesn't have to be complicated or fancy. A simple "Thank You," "Help!" or "I love You, Jesus" will be enough to align your soul with God. It's that simple and that easy.

- -

Jesus, I know You are always with me. I don't want
to ignore You. Show me how to include
You in my life through prayer.

SOUL-LIFE

Always be joyful. Never stop praying. Be thankful in
all circumstances, for this is God's will for you.
1 THESSALONIANS 5:16–18 NLT

These verses don't seem very practical or realistic, do they? *Always* be joyful? *Never* stop praying? Be thankful in *all* circumstances? Really? No one can do that! And yet the Bible says this is God's will for you. So how can you live your life according to these verses?

First, notice that Paul (who wrote these verses) did not say to give thanks *for* all circumstances; he said to give thanks *in* all circumstances. God isn't expecting you to say, "Thank You that I failed that test," or "Thank You that my friend hurt my feelings." But you can say, "God, I failed that test—but thank You that You still love me anyway," or "God, my feelings are so hurt—but thank You that You will never abandon or reject me."

These verses aren't talking about body-life, mind-life, or emotion-life. No one can be happy all the time, and no one can be on their knees in prayer every minute of the day. These words are referring to soul-life. No matter what's going on in your external life, you can always be in a state of joyful connection with God in your soul. You don't have to be consciously praying for the lines of communication between you and God to remain open. And the more you live like that, the more easily you will be able to say "Thank You" to God, even in the middle of the most awful day ever!

God, tonight as I think back on my day, I want to say thank
You. Thank You that You were there with me, through it all.

SWEET DREAMS

*"I make myself known to them in visions
or speak to them in dreams."*

NUMBERS 12:6 GW

. . . .

God has many ways to talk to us, but sometimes we're too busy to listen. We get so preoccupied with our thoughts that it's hard to hear what He's saying. Sometimes, even when we're praying, we may be so busy telling God what we would like to happen that we forget to listen. But God doesn't give up. He keeps on trying to reach us. He wants to tell us how to be happier, how to follow Him more closely, and how to do His work.

One way God talks to people is through their dreams. The Bible is full of stories about people who heard God talking to them in their sleep. This doesn't mean that you'll necessarily hear God's actual voice talking to you in a dream. But you can still pay attention to your dreams. Notice what they might be trying to tell you. God just might be trying to get a message to you!

. . . .

*I want to hear what You have to say to me, God.
Tonight, speak to me through my dreams.
Guide me in the way You want me to go.*

CREATIVITY

*"God has. . .filled him with the Spirit of God, with skill,
ability, and know-how for making all sorts of things,
to design and work in gold, silver, and bronze; to carve
stones and set them; to carve wood, working in every kind
of skilled craft. . . . He's gifted them with the know-how
needed for carving, designing, weaving, and embroidering
in blue, purple, and scarlet fabrics, and in fine linen.
They can make anything and design anything."*
Exodus 35:30–35 msg

. . . .

God is the Creator. Creativity is in His nature. Not only
did He create the world, but He also continues to create
beauty in countless ways. Each flower, each snowflake,
each animal, and each human all express God's creativity.
So do friendships. . .and problems that get resolved. . .and
broken relationships that are healed. The creativity of God
is constantly at work in our world.

You were made in God's image, so that means you too
are a creator. Your soul needs creativity to be healthy. Each
person is creative in her own unique way. Some people write
stories, others paint pictures. Some people dance, while
others are talented actors. Some folks come up with new
ideas in science or math; some design or sew clothes; some
are good at figuring out solutions to problems. Everyone
has *some* form of creativity. Whatever form that takes in
you, think of it as God expressing Himself through you. It
makes Him happy when you join Him in creation.

. . . .

*God, thank You for making me creative.
Please give me a chance tomorrow to use my gifts for You,
because that will make us both happy!*

NATURE

"This is GOD's Message, the God who made earth, made it livable and lasting, known everywhere as GOD: 'Call to me and I will answer you. I'll tell you marvelous and wondrous things that you could never figure out on your own.'"
JEREMIAH 33:2–3 MSG

You don't have to be in a church to feel close to God. Being alone in nature can be an opportunity to feel God's presence with you. In fact, sometimes you may be more intensely aware of God when you're alone outdoors than you ever are during a church service. Whether it's the ocean or the woods, a beautiful sunset or the awesome power of a lightning storm, God often speaks to us through creation. Without using any words, He speaks to our souls.

If your spiritual life has started to feel dry and boring, make a plan to spend some time outside soon. Take a walk in the woods. Go to your favorite park. Or just watch the sunrise from your window tomorrow morning. Let your soul soak up the beauty, and then call out to God. See what He might have to say to you, silently, wordlessly, through the beauty of His creation.

Thank You, God, for Your creation. Tell me marvelous, wondrous things through the world of nature. I want to hear Your voice.

SOULS IN COMMUNITY

*Where two or three are gathered together in my name,
there am I in the midst of them.*

MATTHEW 18:20 KJV

. . . .

Communities are made up of people working together and supporting and helping each other. They can be big or small. Jesus taught His followers how to live together in community. He said that even when there were only two or three people gathered together, He would be there. Our souls—the spiritual part of us—need other people. God uses healthy communities to speak to us and help us grow.

Our community won't be made up of only Christians. Yes, we need the support of other Christians; but God also wants us to form healthy relationships with everyone, Christians and non-Christians alike. Not only does God use us to reach out to others who may not know Him, but He may also use a friendship or a challenging conversation with a non-Christian to speak to our own souls.

When you have some time, read one of the Gospels in the Bible (Matthew, Mark, Luke, or John). You'll see that Jesus repeatedly talked to people who didn't know who He was. He used those conversations, as well as His disciples' relationships with each other, to teach us more about Him.

. . . .

Jesus, thank You that You'll be right there with us tomorrow when my friends and I are together. Use our conversations with each other to bring us all closer to You.

YOUR OWN WAY TO PRAY

"When you pray, go away by yourself, shut the door behind you, and pray to your Father in private."
MATTHEW 6:6 NLT

We need church services and Bible studies or prayer groups. Through church activities, we get support and encouragement. We learn new things about the Bible from people who know more than we do. But as much as we need the church community, we also need to be sure to have our own individual relationships with God. We need to have private conversations with God that only He hears.

God created you with your own unique personality, and He doesn't want you to try to act like your minister or your youth-group leader or anyone else. When you talk to God, remember that He's the only One listening. You can talk to Him however you want, in whatever way seems most natural to you. This is between you and God, no one else. If you feel like singing God a song by your favorite band, go right ahead. Or you could draw Him a picture. You could talk to Him out loud or silently inside your head. You could use words to tell God about your day, or you could let all your words go and simply be in His presence. You could laugh or you could cry. You can be silly or serious. God doesn't care. He only wants to be close to you. Shut your door so no one will see or hear, and just be yourself with God.

Let's spend time together tonight, God. Just You and me.

CONFESSION IS GOOD FOR THE SOUL

Make this your common practice: Confess your sins to each other and pray for each other so that you can live together whole and healed. The prayer of a person living right with God is something powerful to be reckoned with.

JAMES 5:16 MSG

. . . .

To confess means that we admit to someone else that we did something wrong. The very thought of doing this can make us cringe with embarrassment. "Do I really *have* to?" we may ask. After all, God forgives our sins anyway. So why do we have to tell anyone else about them? Can't we just forget about them and move on?

No. Talking to another person about our sins gets them out in the open. It puts them in the light where we can see just how hurtful they are. It allows others to pray for us and with us. They can support us in our struggle to live the faithful life God wants for us.

Confessing your sins to someone you trust doesn't have to be scary or embarrassing. No one's perfect; we all make mistakes. When you tell a friend your sins, she can pray for you; and then when she tells you about the mistakes she's made, *you* can pray for *her*. It goes both ways. It makes both your souls stronger.

You might even find that it helps you sleep better at night!

. . . .

Jesus, show me the right person to confess my sins to. Give me a friend who will pray for me.

PRAYING IN JESUS' NAME

"You did not choose me, but I chose you and appointed
you so that you might go and bear fruit—fruit that
will last—and so that whatever you ask in
my name the Father will give you."
JOHN 15:16 NIV

. . . .

Jesus chose *you*. Before you were even born, He wanted
you to be His friend. He had special work for you to do
and a plan for your life that was meant just for you. As you
live with Him, your soul will expand and grow. Your life will
produce good things, things you can be proud of having
accomplished, things that will please Jesus and help other
people see Him more clearly. You and Jesus will be so close
that you'll be able to ask God to use you in new ways.

But this verse doesn't mean that Jesus' name is like a
magic word that will grant your every wish. If you think of
prayer in that way, you're going to be disappointed. When
you ask something in Jesus' name, you're not asking for
something selfish. You're asking for something that Jesus
wants to happen.

. . . .

Jesus, thank You for choosing me. Thank You that
I can call You my friend. Please use me to do Your
work in the world. As I come to You tonight,
show me how to pray in Your name.

THE SPIRIT IS WITH YOU

God's Spirit is right alongside helping us along. If we don't know how or what to pray, it doesn't matter. He does our praying in and for us, making prayer out of our wordless sighs, our aching groans. He knows us far better than we know ourselves. . .and keeps us present before God. That's why we can be so sure that every detail in our lives of love for God is worked into something good.
ROMANS 8:26–28 MSG

Your spiritual life doesn't have to be hard or complicated. Really, it's simply a question of trusting God's Spirit. It doesn't matter *what* you say when you come to God in prayer; it just matters that you do come to Him. You don't have to know the right thing to say. You don't even have to put your thoughts into words. The Spirit understands you better than you even understand yourself.

And as you make a habit of focusing on God's Spirit in your life, you'll find that your life changes both inside and out. Somehow He'll use every little detail—from the moment your alarm goes off in the morning until you fall asleep at night, and even your dreams while you sleep—to bring good things into your life. He loves you so much!

Spirit of God, thank You that You are with me right now. Take all my thoughts, all my emotions, and all my physical feelings. Turn them all into prayer. Use them to make something good.

DON'T WAIT FOR A CRISIS!

"Stay alert; be in prayer so you don't wander into temptation without even knowing you're in danger. There is a part of you that is eager, ready for anything in God. But there's another part that's as lazy as an old dog sleeping by the fire."

MATTHEW 26:41 MSG

. . . .

Almost everyone prays in a crisis, even people who don't normally care much about God or even believe in Him. When something bad happens, prayer seems to be a normal human instinct. But God doesn't want you to wait until danger strikes before you pray. He wants prayer to be woven through your entire life.

Imagine if you only talked to your closest friend when you were upset and the rest of the time you ignored her. Pretty soon she probably wouldn't be your closest friend anymore. She wouldn't know what was going on in your life most of the time, and you wouldn't know what was going on in hers. She might even feel a little used.

The same idea applies to your relationship with God. Prayer isn't meant to be just for a crisis. God wants you to talk to Him all the time about everything. That way, when something bad does happen, you won't have to shout "Help!" at the top of your lungs, hoping He'll hear you. He'll already be right there beside you.

. . . .

Remind me, God, to talk to You throughout my day tomorrow. Stay close beside me.

FORGIVE OTHERS!

"When you stand praying, if you hold anything against anyone, forgive them, so that your Father in heaven may forgive you your sins."

MARK 11:25 NIV

Have you ever tried to pray when you were angry at someone? It doesn't work very well, does it? Your anger comes between you and God.

But this doesn't mean you should wait until your anger fades away before you have your prayer time. And you don't have to pretend to God that you're not upset when you really are. Instead, you can bring your anger to God. You can ask Him to help you forgive the person who has made you so mad. He can help you see things differently. You'll be able to come close to God with nothing in between you and His Spirit.

That's not always as easy as it sounds of course. Sometimes we want to hold on to our anger. We don't want to let God in because we don't *want* to forgive the other person. That's where this verse comes in. As long as we insist on being angry at someone else, God can't enter into our souls and change them. We must give the anger to Him, and then as He helps us forgive the other person, He also forgives us. He puts our souls back on track.

*When people make me mad, God,
remind me to turn to You. Help me to forgive.*

THE PATH TO GOD

*He refreshes my soul. He guides me
along the right paths for his name's sake.*
PSALM 23:3 NIV

• •

God wants to refresh your soul. To do that, He has created your own personal path to Him.

In Gary Thomas's book *Sacred Pathways*, he wrote that everyone has their own unique way that they've been wired to connect with God. Some people love to worship Him through music, dance, or some other art form. Some people feel closest to God when they're learning and studying, discovering new things about Him. Other folks serve God by helping people in need or by taking a stand to fight what's wrong in the world, and some people long to just sit in silence alone with God. There are people who feel close to God at church, and there are others who sense His presence more closely when they're outdoors in nature. Some people like to be noisy and excited when they worship God, and others prefer calm, quiet moments of prayer.

You may find that *all* these forms of worship help you get to know God better. If there's something on the list you've never considered as a way to spend time with God, try it out. But also make sure you find the way that works *best* for you. Don't feel you have to worship God the way your parents or your pastor or your Sunday school teacher does. Let God lead you on your very own path.

• •

*God, lead me to You.
Show me my special way to worship You.*

ETERNAL LIFE

*Someone may ask, "How will the dead be raised?
What kind of bodies will they have?" What a foolish
question! When you put a seed into the ground, it doesn't
grow into a plant unless it dies first. And what you put in
the ground is not the plant that will grow, but only a bare
seed of wheat or whatever you are planting. Then God
gives it the new body he wants it to have. A different
plant grows from each kind of seed.*
1 CORINTHIANS 15:35–38 NLT

Your soul-life will never end. Even when the time comes
for your body to die, your soul will continue to live.

Some people don't believe that. They say it doesn't
make sense. How can God bring bodies back to life after
they've been buried in the ground for hundreds, even
thousands, of years? And what about people who are
cremated? Will God find all the ashes, somehow turn them
into living cells again, and then put them all back together?

But those questions don't really matter. Eternal life
is a mystery too big for us to understand. And when you
think about it, do you understand how a seed—a tiny little
thing inside a hard shell—is able to grow into a tall, green
plant? Does that make any sense either?

Your soul is like a seed. You can't even imagine how
it will grow in eternity. But you can trust God that it will
be amazing.

*Death is scary, God. I don't understand how my soul
can live forever. But I trust You. Thank You
that You know what You are doing.*

PRAISE

Praise the LORD, my soul; all my inmost being,
praise his holy name.
PSALM 103:1 NIV

Again and again, the Bible tells us to praise God. But what does that really mean? Does God want us to say nice things about Him all the time so that He'll feel better about Himself? No, of course not! God doesn't get insecure. He doesn't have a bad concept of Himself the way we sometimes do of ourselves. God wants us to praise Him because He knows it's good for our souls.

To praise God means to celebrate His kindness and love. It means that we express our love for God either in words or actions (or both). Doing this turns our attention away from life's gloom and doom. It helps us look at life from a different perspective so that we see God's hand at work. It's a way to draw closer to God. It allows Him the freedom to act in our souls and in our lives.

You can praise God in all sorts of ways. In prayer, yes, but also by singing, by clapping your hands, by jumping up and down with joy, by dancing, by writing a poem, or by painting a picture. We praise God with our bodies, with our minds and thoughts, with our emotions, and with our actions. All these forms of praise help our souls grow.

Show me how to praise You, God,
now before I sleep and throughout the day tomorrow.
May everything I do celebrate You.

WAIT FOR GOD

My soul waits in silence for God only;
from Him is my salvation.
PSALM 62:1 NASB

. . . .

Sometimes words fail us. We don't know what to say. We don't even know what to think. But we can still pray, even in silence, even when our minds have gone blank. In fact, those are the very moments when God may be able to reach us most clearly. When we finally stop talking, when we simply wait to see what God will do next, without any demands, then He can surprise us in new ways.

Don't try to deny or avoid the emptiness you feel inside sometimes. Instead, allow it to carve out space in your soul for you to receive more of God's presence. Let the truth of who you are surface during these empty moments of silence; be willing to face the reality of the person you are, flaws and all. Then remember that God loves you unconditionally just as you are. He is with you. He is in you. He is *for* you. He will do something wonderful in your life. Just wait and see!

. . . .

Show me, God, whatever I need to see—about myself
and about You—and help me to be patient
enough to wait for You.

HOLY

May the God of peace make you holy in every way,
and may your whole spirit and soul and body be kept
blameless until our Lord Jesus Christ comes again.

1 Thessalonians 5:23 nlt

. . . .

When the Bible says that God wants to make you "holy in
every way," it doesn't mean that He wants to turn you into
a religious goody-goody. In the original Greek language
in which this verse was written, the word translated as
holy meant literally "to be set apart as different." In other
words, to be holy is to be different from the world around
you. It means you think differently, and you act differently.
You belong to God, and you are the unique, special person
He created you to be. Yes, maybe some people will think
that "different" means "weird"—but that's okay, because
they don't understand everything that God is doing in you.

The word *holy* in this verse also has to do with being
whole and healthy, without any rotten spots or guilt, right
down to the very center of your being. This is what the
God of peace—the God of safety and wholeness—will do
for your soul if you let Him. In fact, He's already doing it
right now, tonight!

. . . .

Make me whole, God. Take out anything spoiled or broken.
Make me the special person You want me to be.

BOASTING ABOUT GOD

This is what the LORD says: Don't let wise people brag about their wisdom. . . . If they want to brag, they should brag that they understand and know me. They should brag that I, the LORD, act out of love, righteousness, and justice on the earth. This kind of bragging pleases me, declares the LORD.
JEREMIAH 9:23-24 GW

. . . .

Do you understand who God is? Do you really know Him? Here are some Bible verses to think about tonight, verses that tell you what God is like:

- Psalm 90:2; Romans 1:20; 1 Timothy 1:17—God is eternal.
- Psalm 139:7-12—God is present everywhere, at all times.
- Psalm 139:1-6; Matthew 6:8; 1 John 3:20—God knows everything that happens.
- Psalm 115:3; Matthew 19:26; Luke 1:37—Nothing is impossible for God.
- Matthew 19:17—God is good.
- Psalm 136; John 3:16; 1 John 4:15-16—God is love.
- Psalm 32:1-2; 86:5; 103:3—God is forgiving.
- Psalm 31:5; 89:8; Lamentations 3:23—God keeps promises.

Most of all, spend some time at night reading Matthew, Mark, Luke, and John. These are the books of the Bible that will tell you about the life of Jesus, and Jesus is the best way to know God!

. . . .

*Jesus, help me to get to know You more and more.
Then I can boast about how wonderful You are!*

COUNTING ON JESUS

If I know the law but still can't keep it, and if the power of sin within me keeps sabotaging my best intentions, I obviously need help! I realize that I don't have what it takes. I can will it, but I can't do it. I decide to do good, but I don't really do it; I decide not to do bad, but then I do it anyway. My decisions, such as they are, don't result in actions. Something has gone wrong deep within me and gets the better of me every time. . . . I've tried everything and nothing helps. I'm at the end of my rope. Is there no one who can do anything for me? Isn't that the real question? The answer, thank God, is that Jesus Christ can and does. He acted to set things right in this life of contradictions.

ROMANS 7:17-20, 24-25 MSG

. . . .

We've all felt the way this verse describes—we want to do good but then we don't. We make up our minds to live differently, and then we fall back into old habits. It's so frustrating and so discouraging. After a while, we may want to give up. But when we keep coming back to Jesus, telling Him our mistakes and asking His Spirit to help us do better, He can and will help us change. It may not happen as quickly as we might wish, but we must keep our eyes fixed on Jesus no matter what.

. . . .

*Jesus, I'm counting on You to change me.
I can't do it myself.*

DON'T LIE TO YOURSELF!

*If we say, "We have a relationship with God" and yet live in
the dark, we're lying. We aren't being truthful. But if we live
in the light in the same way that God is in the light,
we have a relationship with each other. . . . If we say,
"We aren't sinful" we are deceiving ourselves,
and the truth is not in us.*

1 JOHN 1:6–8 GW

Sometimes it can seem like sin refers to anything in God's
Word that is a "don't." But that's not what the Bible means
when it talks about sin. Sin is anything—whether thoughts or
actions—that makes us turn away from God and each other.
It's putting ourselves first, ahead of anything and anyone.

All of us fall into sin. Sooner or later we turn from
God and one another. We hurt others. We deny the God
who loves us. But when we do, we need to turn back to
Him as soon as possible. That's what it means to repent—it
means to turn around. When we do, He's already waiting
there, hands held out to make us clean again. Nothing can
separate us from God's love. Not even sin.

*As I look back at my day, I see the places where
I turned away from You and the people around
me—the places where I put myself first.
Forgive me, God, for my sin and selfishness.*

WAITING

*Because of the LORD's faithful love we do not perish,
for His mercies never end. They are new every morning;
great is Your faithfulness! I say: The LORD is my portion,
therefore I will put my hope in Him. The LORD is good to
those who wait for Him, to the person who seeks Him.
It is good to wait quietly for deliverance from the LORD.*
LAMENTATIONS 3:22–26 HCSB

. . . .

It's hard to wait. Sometimes we must wait to be old enough
to do something. We may have to wait until we have enough
money. We have to wait until our parents give us permission
to do something. We sometimes have to wait until we've
learned the skills we need.

God has plans for everything, but not everything
may be ready yet. Sometimes we must wait until God has
everything prepared. We must trust He knows the right
time. We must learn to wait for God's perfect timing.

In the meantime, we can know that God *does* have
something new to give us every single day.

. . . .

*Thank You, God, that You know the right time for
everything. I'm looking forward to whatever
You want to show me tomorrow.*

GOD WON'T EVER GIVE UP ON YOU!

I am sure of this, that He who started a good work in you will carry it on to completion.

PHILIPPIANS 1:6 HCSB

. . . .

Do you ever feel impatient with yourself? Do you wonder, *Why can't I have more self-confidence? Why am I so shy? Why do I keep making the same mistakes? Why can't I be more like so-and-so? Why do I cry so easily? Why do I keep losing my temper? When will I learn to act differently?*

God wants you to give all those questions to Him and then trust Him. He is helping you to grow and mature in so many ways, including your body, mind, emotions, and most of all, your soul. He's not going to forget to finish the job that He's begun in you!

The Holy Spirit knows how fast you can grow. You may want to push yourself faster, but the Spirit knows what's best for you. Trust His timing.

. . . .

Spirit of God, thank You that You always know what I need most. When I feel impatient with myself, help me to trust You. I'm so glad that You will never stop helping me grow.

SOUL ENERGY

Be energetic in your life of salvation, reverent and sensitive before God. That energy is God's energy, an energy deep within you, God himself willing and working at what will give him the most pleasure.

PHILIPPIANS 2:12–13 MSG

. . . .

How can you be energetic in your Christian life? Well, think about what gives your body energy. Two of the most important things are eating and breathing. So, when it comes to your soul-life, you need to "eat" by reading your Bible and learning more about God. And you "breathe" by praying. Some people even recommend connecting your body's breath with a prayer. Here are some short, simple prayers you can repeat in the space of a breath:

- I can't. *(Breathe in.)* You can. *(Breathe out.)*
- Help me be still. *(Breathe in.)* You are God. *(Breathe out.)*
- Here I am. *(Breathe in.)* Use me. *(Breathe out.)*
- I love You. *(Breathe in.)* I know You love me. *(Breathe out.)*
- Not what I want. *(Breathe in.)* What You want. *(Breathe out.)*
- Show me Your way. *(Breathe in.)* I want to follow You. *(Breathe out.)*

Practice making these "breath prayers" a part of your daily life, and you'll find you have a lot more "soul energy."

. . . .

God, thank You that Your Spirit is working inside me already. Remind me to "breathe" You in not just tonight but also throughout my day tomorrow.

PRACTICE LOVE, NOT SIN

People conceived and brought into life by God don't make a practice of sin. How could they? God's seed is deep within them, making them who they are. It's not in the nature of the God-begotten to practice and parade sin. Here's how you tell the difference between God's children and the Devil's children: The one who won't practice righteous ways isn't from God, nor is the one who won't love brother or sister. A simple test.

1 JOHN 3:9–10 MSG

. . . .

We all make mistakes. We all sin. No matter how long we've been following Jesus, we fall short of what He wants for us. We put ourselves first. We act selfishly, and we hurt others. We turn away from God.

That's a fact of life, at least life on this side of eternity, but it's not an excuse for making a *habit* out of sinning. We can't say to ourselves, *Oh, it doesn't matter if I keep sinning day after day because God will forgive me.*

Instead, no matter how many times we slip up, we keep practicing love for God and others. We keep trying, day after day, until love becomes a habit. We let God's seeds in our souls sprout and grow, and one day they will blossom and bear fruit.

. . . .

*God, I don't want to make a habit of sinning.
Remind me tomorrow, as many times as
I need reminding, to practice love.*

YOU'RE A NEW PERSON!

Anyone who belongs to Christ has become a new person.
The old life is gone; a new life has begun!
2 CORINTHIANS 5:17 NLT

. . . .

Being a "new person" doesn't mean that after you decide to follow Jesus, you magically turn into someone else. You're still you. You'll still have all your own unique quirkiness, and you will still struggle with your flaws and failures.

Some people say that the decision to give your life to Jesus is like signing a contract with someone to remodel your house. The work won't all be done at once. You still may have to live with leaky faucets and cracks in the floor, but the work *will* get done.

Becoming a new person in Jesus also means you give everything to Him. You give Him permission to come in and do whatever work needs to be done in your soul. Sure, you will still make mistakes, but your overall attitude toward life has changed. Now Jesus is in charge.

And that changes everything!

. . . .

Jesus, I'm excited about the new
life You and I are sharing.

SET FREE

Live freely, animated and motivated by God's Spirit.
Then you won't feed the compulsions of selfishness.
For there is a root of sinful self-interest in us that is at
odds with a free spirit, just as the free spirit is incompatible
with selfishness. These two ways of life are antithetical,
so that you cannot live at times one way and at times
another way according to how you feel on any given
day. Why don't you choose to be led by the Spirit?
GALATIANS 5:16–18 MSG

The more we let the Spirit lead us, the less we will fall back into our old selfish ways of living. Left on our own, we naturally focus on our own lives and our own interests. We put ourselves first. But the more we connect our souls to God's Spirit, the more He can change us.

Your nightly prayer time is a good opportunity to let the Spirit into your life, but so is every other moment of the day! It literally takes only a second to open your soul and mind and ask Him to set you free from your selfishness.

Spirit, I don't want to keep being so selfish. Come into me.
Change me. Set me free from myself. I want to love
You every minute of every day, and I want to
show Your love to everyone around me.

THE SOUL'S FRUIT

*What happens when we live God's way? He brings gifts
into our lives, much the same way that fruit appears in an
orchard—things like affection for others, exuberance about
life, serenity. We develop a willingness to stick with
things, a sense of compassion in the heart.*

GALATIANS 5:22 MSG

. . . .

We have to make up our minds to follow Jesus. Once
we've done that, we have to decide to *keep* following Him
day after day, moment by moment. God won't make the
decision for us. He will never force us to do something
we don't want to do.

Once you make that decision, He can take over. He'll
make your life grow and bear soul-fruit. Just as an apple tree
doesn't have to concentrate hard and grunt and groan in
order to grow apples, you won't have to work to produce
God's soul-fruit (things like love, joy, peace, endurance,
compassion for others). It will just happen naturally.

. . . .

*Jesus, I've made up my mind to follow You. Send Your
Spirit into my soul. Make me grow and bear Your fruit.*

THE LOVE OF JESUS

I am like a flourishing pine tree;
your fruit comes from Me.
HOSEA 14:8 HCSB

. . . .

The Bible has a lot to say about the "fruit of the Spirit." Galatians 5:22–23 says the fruit of the Spirit is love, joy, peace, patience, kindness, goodness, faith, gentleness, and self-control. These are the qualities that will just naturally grow out from our souls when God's Spirit of love is at work in us.

Imagine that God is like a green, healthy evergreen tree growing deep inside you. His life and your life have been merged together. Your life will begin more and more to be an expression of God.

Or you could say that the fruit of the Spirit is the love of Jesus flowing into us and out of us to others. Through Jesus, we have God's living presence in us, and this means we become more and more like Him.

. . . .

Make me more and more open to You, Jesus, so that I don't
do anything to block the flow of Your love. Let it move
through me freely so that You and I become closer
and closer. May my life bear Your fruit. Tomorrow,
use me to touch everyone I see with Your love.

Your Friends and Family

GOD'S HOME

*In him you too are being built together to become
a dwelling in which God lives by his Spirit.*
EPHESIANS 2:22 NIV

God speaks to you both as an individual and as a member
of the community the Bible calls the body of Christ. Your
private alone time tonight with God is strengthening you
to be a part of the body tomorrow. As you soak up His
love now, you'll have more love to pass along to others
tomorrow. When you express God's love by encouraging
others, sharing their joy, helping them when they need
something, and being kind to them when they're feeling
sad or lonely, you're drawing from the love God's giving
you now in your alone time.

You are an essential, necessary part of Christ's body.
You are needed. Together—you and all the rest of us—are
being built into a community where God's Spirit can feel
at home.

*Jesus, thank You that I'm a part of Your body. Fill me
with Your Spirit now, while we are alone together,
so that I can share You with others tomorrow.
I want to help You build a place where
You can live in us.*

FOLLOW THE LEADER

You who are younger must follow your leaders. But all of you, leaders and followers alike, are to be down to earth with each other, for—God has had it with the proud, but takes delight in just plain people.

1 PETER 5:5 MSG

When we were little, we probably liked playing Follow the Leader, but as adolescents, the game's no longer much fun. We can see all too clearly that our leaders aren't perfect. Whether it's our teachers, our parents, or our government, we now recognize they make mistakes. We don't want to follow them blindly, and God doesn't want us to. But we need to ask ourselves: "Am I feeling rebellious toward the leaders in my life because I think they're steering me in the wrong direction, or is it because I want to be in control?" God asks us to be humble enough to accept direction.

Ultimately, it is God we are to follow. Often, He does use our leaders to guide us, but if we're certain that's not the case, then God's will for us comes first. But be careful. Don't rush into rebellion. Pray about it first. And pray that God will use and bless your leaders.

God, help me have the humility I need to accept direction. Remind me to be open to learning from those who have more experience than I do. I ask Your blessing on the leaders in my life. Guide them with Your wisdom.

IT'S NOT FAIR!

*Do not fret because of those who are evil
or be envious of those who do wrong.*

PSALM 37:1 NIV

. . . .

Sometimes life doesn't seem fair. We watch our friends or siblings get away with things, and we feel jealous and resentful. Maybe they boast or post something unkind on Facebook or some other social-media app, and then they get a hundred or so thumbs-ups, hearts, and smiley faces. Meanwhile, we're quietly trying to do our best, and no one seems to notice.

Try not to think too much about things like this. Don't give people the power to ruin your day or spoil the contentment God wants you to experience. Instead, say a quick prayer, putting the entire situation in God's hands, and then move on. Remember that God has a very specific and personal plan for you. You don't need to feel jealous of anyone!

. . . .

*You know, God, that sometimes I wish I could get away
with things like some of my friends do. I hate to admit it,
but it's true. I wish people would give me attention, even if
it's for doing things You don't want me to do. Right now,
tonight, I'm giving all my envy and upset feelings to
You. Help me to focus on You and not worry so
much about what my friends are doing.*

THE GOLDEN RULE

"Treat others the same way you
want them to treat you."
LUKE 6:31 NASB

. . . .

This verse is also called the Golden Rule. It's a rule-of-thumb guide for how you interact with your friends and family. It makes following Jesus pretty simple.

When we follow the Golden Rule, we don't do it to impress others. We're not being nice to them so that they'll be nice to us. We don't think that if we act a certain way with our friends and family, we'll get something back. All those reasons are ultimately selfish.

The Golden Rule means different things in different situations. It might mean that since we like to be complimented and supported by our friends, we go out of our way to compliment and support them. It could mean that because we like to be listened to when we speak, we're careful to pay attention when our friends and family are talking to us. Or it could mean that in the same way that we want to be forgiven after we've hurt someone, we are quick to forgive others who hurt us.

Following the Golden Rule isn't about getting anything back. It's about giving to others the same way that Jesus gives to us.

. . . .

Jesus, tomorrow as I go through my day,
remind me to treat everyone the way I want to be
treated. Help me to act the way You would.

TEAM PLAYER

*"Don't be afraid of them. Put your minds on the Master,
great and awesome, and then fight for your brothers,
your sons, your daughters, your wives, and your homes."*
NEHEMIAH 4:14 MSG

. . . .

Imagine you're out on a playing field with your team. You look at the opposing team, and you see that they're tall, muscular, and fast. So, you turn around, walk off the field, and go home.

You wouldn't do that, would you? So, don't do it to your friends and family when they're up against a tough situation. Stand by them. Support them. Encourage them.

God knows that we need each other. Just as you need your friends and family, they need you. Together, you can handle things that you might be too weak to cope with on your own. You can combine your talents and lean on each other.

Most of all, we can pray for each other. When we allow God to be on our team, the game turns around!

. . . .

*Make me a loyal friend and family member, God.
May I show others the same love and support You show
me. Forgive me for the times I haven't been the friend
You want me to be. Help me to follow Your example.*

LET GO OF THAT GRUDGE!

"If you enter your place of worship and, about to make an offering, you suddenly remember a grudge a friend has against you, abandon your offering, leave immediately, go to this friend and make things right. Then and only then, come back and work things out with God."
MATTHEW 5:23–24 MSG

It's hard to let go of grudges sometimes. *After all,* we tell ourselves, *I'm right and the other person is wrong. I'm not the one who's out of line. He is.* When Jesus spoke the words in today's verses, though, He knew that our anger at a friend or family member can come between our hearts and His. A grudge acts like a wall, shutting us up inside ourselves where we can no longer talk to God.

So tonight, if you realize you're holding on to a grudge, let it go. You can do it right now. Send a quick text message or email saying you're sorry. Make things right. With that out of the way, you and God can enjoy your quiet time together.

Jesus, give me the strength to let go of grudges.
You know that my anger and resentment hurt me
as much as they do anyone else. I don't want to
let anything come between You and me.
Show me what I need to do or
say to make things right.

PERFECT LOVE

*Rather, perfect love gets rid of fear, because fear
involves punishment. The person who lives
in fear doesn't have perfect love.*

1 JOHN 4:18 GW

When we truly believe someone loves us, we're not afraid
that person will hurt us. Love makes us feel secure because
real love is kind. If someone says they love you, but they
keep hurting you—either physically or verbally—then they
don't *really* love you. You deserve better.

God doesn't want you to be in relationships that make
you feel bad about yourself. He doesn't want you to spend
time with someone you're afraid will do you harm. You're
His special daughter, and He wants only good things for you.

If someone is hurting you—whether it's a parent, another adult, a friend, a boyfriend, or anyone—tell someone
you can trust. Get help. Ask God to show you whom to
talk to. Ask Him to heal your wounded heart.

*Thank You, God, that Your love is perfect.
You will never hurt me.*

GENTLE WORDS

A gentle answer deflects anger,
but harsh words make tempers flare.
PROVERBS 15:1 NLT

. . . .

Words are powerful. We can all remember hurtful words that were spoken to us, sometimes even years ago. "You're stupid!" "You're fat!" "You're clumsy!" Words like that, especially when spoken by the people we care about most, can leave lasting scars. No wonder that we're quick to respond to these words with anger. We want to defend ourselves. But when we do that, it's often like pouring gasoline on sparks—it makes the situation explode into something even more destructive than it was.

Jesus' advice to His followers was to do nothing when they were hurt. That's how He acted when His friend betrayed Him. That seems like really bad advice, but Jesus put Himself in His Father's hands so that God's love could flow out through Him into the world. And we can do the same.

. . . .

Jesus, You know that the things people say to me
sometimes hurt me so deeply. Tonight, as I look back at the
scars I bear from others' words, help me to give each one
of those wounds to You. Teach me to be more like You.
Help me to love even when I'm hurt. Help my words
be gentle even when others speak harshly to
me. Thank You for always loving me.

TROLLS

Never pay back evil for evil to anyone.
Respect what is right.
ROMANS 12:17 NASB

. . . .

Following Jesus while we're on the internet is one of the greatest challenges we face today. Dealing with "trolls"—people who are rude and mean on social media—can be especially hard. Most of these people wouldn't ever talk like that to our faces, and yet something about the internet makes us all feel as though we don't have to follow the normal rules for polite, grown-up behavior.

How should we respond when our friends turn into trolls? First, don't feed the trolls. In other words, don't take their bait. Don't get into an online argument. Ignore their ugly words. Second, try to see past the words. What's motivating them? If you express sympathy and understanding for the underlying hurt, trolls often turn back into human beings. And finally, pray for them. Ask the peace of Jesus to come into their hearts.

. . . .

Jesus, when my social media friends act like trolls, remind me that I don't have to sink to their level. Instead, use me to carry Your love on the internet. Give me the wisdom to know when to respond and when to ignore. Heal the hurt and insecurity that makes people act like trolls.

THE GIFT OF SEX

Don't let sexual sin, perversion of any kind,
or greed even be mentioned among you. This is not
appropriate behavior for God's holy people.
EPHESIANS 5:3 GW

Sex is a gift from God, so if anyone tries to tell you that it's bad, don't believe them. But as with everything else in life, there's a time to say no and a time to say yes. As a teenager, when you say no to sex, you're protecting yourself. You're also protecting the other person in the relationship. You're saying no to sex, but you're saying yes to physical health and emotional security. You're saying yes to what God wants for your life. God wants you to be safe, emotionally and physically—and the safest place for sex is within a committed marriage relationship. (It's worth the wait!)

Notice that today's verse says that we're not even to mention this kind of sin. That doesn't mean we shouldn't talk about our temptations and ask for support. What it does mean is that we're not to talk about sex in a way that doesn't honor others or ourselves. You may not actually be engaging in sexual intercourse, but you can talk about sex in a way that cheapens it or in a way that turns other human beings into objects. You don't want to be treated that way, so don't treat others that way either.

God, thank You for the gift of sex. You know
and understand my body's needs. Help me to say
no now so that I can say yes to all that You
have planned for me in the future.

GOSSIPING HURTS!

"You must not pass along false rumors."
EXODUS 23:1 NLT

. . . .

We've all been guilty of gossiping. It seems pretty harmless—and it can be such fun! But the Bible takes gossip very seriously. In the book of Romans, gossip is included in a list of other sins, alongside murder, greed, lying, and cruelty. Gossip has the power to hurt and destroy. It's not the innocent, forgivable pastime we like to imagine it is.

Gossip betrays our relationships with others. It puts them at risk by hurting their reputations. When you realize that you and your friends are slipping into gossip, here are three responses:

- Walk away. Don't stick around and get sucked into the conversation.
- Say something positive. Turn the conversation around by saying something nice about the person.
- Speak up. Tell your friends that you don't want to gossip.

You wouldn't want to know your friends were talking about you behind your back, so don't do it to them!

. . . .

Remind me tomorrow, God, that gossiping is hurtful.
Give me the courage and determination not
to participate in talking about others.

LOVE IS A CHOICE

*Love is patient and kind. Love is not jealous or boastful
or proud or rude. It does not demand its own way.
It is not irritable, and it keeps no record of
being wronged. . . . Love never gives up.*
1 Corinthians 13:4–5, 7 nlt

. . . .

We often think that love is an emotion, a feeling. We "fall in love." We "love" pizza and our favorite band and sparkly nail polish. But that's not the kind of love the Bible talks about.

The love these verses are focusing on has to do with how you act and think. It's not a feeling. It's a choice. It's a way you *decide* to act. This kind of love is about giving, not receiving. It's the love expressed by the Golden Rule, which looks out for the other person's interests as though they were your own.

Try turning these verses from the Bible into a prayer. Ask God to make these actions and attitudes a daily part of your life.

. . . .

*Jesus, help me be patient and kind to my friends and
family. Help me not be jealous or boastful or proud or rude.
Remind me not to demand my own way. Help me not be
irritable. Help me to forgive and forget when I'm hurt.
I ask that You help me to never give up on the people I love.*

YOUR IDENTITY

*Now, this is what the LORD says: Do not be afraid,
because I have reclaimed you. I have called
you by name; you are mine.*

ISAIAH 43:1 GW

. . . .

It's hard to interact with the people we care about when
we're not sure of our own identity. When we lack confidence in our own worth, we're often too easily influenced
by others. We may get our feelings hurt too easily. It's hard
to be a good friend when we aren't certain who we are.

So, who are you? Do you know? Are you sure of your
own identity? The answers to these questions don't always
come easily. You'll probably continue to find out new things
about yourself for the rest of your life. At the most basic,
unchanging level, here's who you are: You are God's child.
Through Jesus, you have the same relationship with God
that Jesus does. God loves you.

That is your identity!

. . . .

*Thank You, God, that my identity is safe with You. When I'm
not certain of who I am, when I lack confidence in myself
or I don't like myself very much, remind me that You love
me. Tomorrow, help me to live in a way that expresses
my true identity to my friends and family. Use me
to show others who they are in You too.*

THE VINE AND THE BRANCHES

"Live in me, and I will live in you. A branch cannot produce any fruit by itself. It has to stay attached to the vine. In the same way, you cannot produce fruit unless you live in me."

JOHN 15:4 GW

. . . .

Do you ever wonder if you're *really* a Christian? Do you ask yourself, *How can I call myself a Christian when I make so many mistakes? How can I say that I'm a follower of Jesus when I keep doing things He doesn't want me to do?*

But following Jesus isn't about what you do and how well you do it. Being a real Christian isn't just following a bunch of rules perfectly. It's about having a living, active relationship with Jesus.

Think about your relationships with human beings. You and your siblings probably fight, but you're still in the same family. Your friends and you may also squabble, yet you keep being friends. The relationship is stronger than the day-to-day ups and downs. As the relationship endures, the better you're able to get along. You understand each other better. You change and grow into better people.

When you're in a relationship with Jesus, it will change you even more than your relationships with other people. You will naturally become more like Him. You'll bear fruit—your life will be filled with love, kindness, peace, and joy—because you're connected to Him.

. . . .

Jesus, thank You that You're the Vine that gives me life. Keep me connected to You so that I can be more like You.

STRENGTH IS FOR SERVICE

Those of us who are strong and able in the faith need to step in and lend a hand to those who falter, and not just do what is most convenient for us.
Strength is for service, not status.
ROMANS 15:1 MSG

. . . .

Sometimes, others' mistakes and weaknesses can make us feel better about ourselves. We look around and think, *Wow, I'm doing so much better than my sister (or brother or friends)!* Maybe we think to ourselves, *I may have my problems, but at least I'm not as bad as they are!*

But God doesn't want us to take pride in our strength compared to others' weaknesses. He gives us our strength so we can use it to help others. Whether we're better at math, have an easier time trusting God, or have more confidence in social situations, we can use our abilities to reach out and help those who aren't as strong in those areas.

Besides, the Bible also says, "Pride goes. . .before a fall" (Proverbs 16:18 NIV). So, we should be careful! We may be feeling strong today, but tomorrow we could be all too aware of our weakness, and then we'll be needing a friend to reach out a hand to help *us*.

. . . .

God, show me ways I can use my strengths to help others tomorrow. Remind me not to pat myself on the back or look down on others' weaknesses.

YOU AND YOUR PARENTS

Children, obey your parents in the Lord,
for this is right. "Honor your father and mother."
EPHESIANS 6:1-2 WEB

. . . .

Since the day you were born, God has used your parents to teach you and guide you. They taught you so many things you needed to know, from how to get along with others to how to tie your shoes. But now that you're an adolescent, you may find that it's harder to fall in line with what your parents want. You want to be in control of your own life, yet God tells you to still obey and honor your parents.

Jesus comes first, and nothing—not even your parents—should come between you and Him. Keeping that in mind, here are some things you can do to demonstrate honor to your parents:

- Speak to them respectfully.
- Do the chores that are your responsibility without complaining.
- Follow your parents' rules, such as curfew and the behaviors allowed in your home.

You can pray for your parents. Parents are human beings with problems of their own. They're not perfect—no one is. But your love and prayers can help encourage them to be the people God wants them to be.

. . . .

God, when my parents seem unfair and unreasonable,
remind me that You want me to honor them. Help me
to forgive them for their failures. Show me ways to
support them and make their lives a little
easier. May they see You in me.

BICKERING

Where do you think all these appalling wars and quarrels
come from? Do you think they just happen? Think again.
They come about because you want your own way,
and fight for it deep inside yourselves.
JAMES 4:1 MSG

. . . .

Do you and the other people in your family argue a lot?
It's easy to get annoyed by the people we share a house
with. Bickering over who gets to use the bathroom first
can quickly turn into a larger and more hurtful argument.
Fighting and arguing can become an ongoing habit, the
constant background to our home lives. When we stop to
think about it, it's hard to see how we're to blame. The fights
just seem to keep happening. They're almost automatic.

If that's the case, then there's something bigger going
on. God wants us to stop and look at ourselves. All those
tiny quarrels that keep escalating into an ongoing war start
inside our own hearts. We want our own way. We want to
be the one who uses the bathroom first. . .or who gets to
choose what we watch on television. . .or who can get out
of household chores.

Here's another place where the Golden Rule comes
in handy. When we really treat the people in our home the
way we would want to be treated, all that bickering comes
to an end pretty quickly!

. . . .

God, show me tonight where my own selfishness
has been causing quarrels in my family.

CARRYING EACH OTHER'S BURDENS

Help carry each other's burdens.
In this way you will follow Christ's teachings.
GALATIANS 6:2 GW

What does it mean to carry our friends' burdens? First, it means to pay attention to what's going on in our friends' lives. If we're too preoccupied with our own problems, we won't notice that our friends may need help. Second, we carry each other's burdens by expressing sympathy and support. We don't just fake it or pretend to care; we genuinely hurt for our friends. We want to do whatever we can to help. That means we don't make excuses for ourselves by thinking, *I've got my own problems to worry about* or *I'm just too busy to help, even though I'd like to.* Instead, we make time to lend a helping hand wherever we can. That may mean we simply listen to our friend and let her unload her feelings. It could mean that we talk through a problem with her, helping her see her options. We might need to loan her something of ours—money, clothes, an iPad, or whatever—so that she has what she needs to deal with whatever her situation is.

By carrying our friends' burdens, we act like Jesus. We treat our friends with the same love and compassion He gives to us.

Jesus, help me show my friends Your love.
Use me to be Your hands in their lives.

WHAT ARE YOU GOING TO WEAR TOMORROW?

So, chosen by God for this new life of love, dress in the wardrobe God picked out for you: compassion, kindness, humility, quiet strength, discipline. Be even-tempered, content with second place, quick to forgive an offense. Forgive as quickly and completely as the Master forgave you. And regardless of what else you put on, wear love. It's your basic, all-purpose garment. Never be without it.
COLOSSIANS 3:12–14 MSG

. . . .

These verses are a good summary of how God wants you to interact with the people around you—with compassion, kindness, humility, and quiet strength. . .not pushing to the head of the line, not always wanting to be in first place. . .quick to forgive when your feelings are hurt. The word *discipline* that's used in this version of the Bible is translated as *patient* in other versions. The original word used in Greek means the willingness to put up with things without giving in to anger. It also means to keep on going and not give up.

All these qualities are summed up with one single word: *love!* God wants you to clothe yourself in love.

. . . .

Tomorrow, as I get dressed, God, remind me to also put on Your wardrobe—compassion, kindness, humbleness, patience. In every conversation, I want to wear Your love.

CRITICISM

*Wounds from a sincere friend are better
than many kisses from an enemy.*

PROVERBS 27:6 NLT

. . . .

We don't like criticism. It hurts. It makes us see ourselves in ways we'd rather not. Unfortunately, in the heat of the moment, we may react with defensive, angry words. But as the Bible points out, a friend's honest feedback can be good for us. How else could we identify some of our own weaknesses, the things we don't want to face about ourselves?

Here are some tips for handling a friend's criticism:

- Stop. Don't react at all! Give yourself time to respond without anger.
- Allow yourself to feel curious. What new thing could you learn about yourself?
- Listen. Be open to what your friend has to say. Don't interrupt.
- Ask questions. Ask your friend to explain anything you don't understand.
- Say thank you. Let your friend know that you appreciate that she cared about you enough to tell you the truth.

God can use our friends to teach us things He wants us to hear, so it makes sense to listen!

. . . .

*God, I don't like to be criticized. Help me to be so secure
in Your love that I can hear the truth about myself,
knowing that nothing will ever make You love me less.*

WHAT KIND OF FRIEND ARE YOU?

Two people are better off than one, for they can help each
other succeed. If one person falls, the other can reach out
and help. But someone who falls alone is in real trouble.
ECCLESIASTES 4:9–10 NLT

. . . .

Life isn't meant to be lived alone. We need other people
in all sorts of ways. We especially need friends. They
keep us company when we're lonely. They can help us
be our best selves. They support us and encourage us
when we're feeling weak. We love the friends who make
us laugh, the ones who make everything seem fun; but
the people we can count on to be there when we're in
trouble are the best kind of friends.

Not only do we want to *have* these kinds of friends,
but God also wants us to *be* this kind of friend—the sort
of friend who sticks around through thick and thin. Take
a moment to jot down all the things you most appreciate
in a friend. Once you've done that, go through each item
of your list and ask yourself: *How good am I at being this*
kind of friend?

If you find there are places you need to improve, ways
you could be a better friend, ask God to help you.

. . . .

Thank You, God, for my friends. Thank You for all the ways
they make my life better. Help me to be a better friend
to them. Show me where I need to change.

PUT YOUR LIFE ON THE LINE

"This is my command: Love one another the way I loved you. This is the very best way to love. Put your life on the line for your friends."
JOHN 15:12–13 MSG

. . . .

The Bible tells us over and over to love others. Jesus showed us with His life what love looks like. He gave away His life for His friends. He did this day by day, in ordinary ways, such as when He talked to people even when He was tired or busy, and He also did it literally, by dying on the cross.

You probably won't be asked to literally die for your friends, but you can put your friends ahead of your own self-centered wants. You can die to your selfishness.

This isn't just something to think about. It doesn't have very much to do with your emotions. You don't have to work up a "love feeling" in order to obey Jesus' words. Instead, take some time to figure out ways you could put your love for your friends into action. What could you do to help make their lives a little easier? Ask Jesus to show you how you can put your life on the line for your friends.

And don't be afraid to ask for help when you need it. Friendship goes two ways!

. . . .

Jesus, show me now something I can do tomorrow to put Your love into action—and then remind me to carry through.

LOYALTY

*Friends love through all kinds of weather,
and families stick together in all kinds of trouble.*
PROVERBS 17:17 MSG

. . . .

In today's online world, it's easy to hang out on our computers and our phones. We can spend so much time looking at social media, watching videos of cute kittens, catching up on our favorite celebrities, and laughing at silly memes that we can forget that real-life relationships take work. We may even forget that when we're online, we're still in touch with *real* people, and we have a responsibility to act in love with them, just as we would if we were interacting in person.

True friends support each other no matter what. They stick up for each other online, in text messages, and in person—and they do it in good times and bad. The same is true for families. Sure, you and your family members may argue; but when it comes right down to it, make sure you have their backs. Be loyal!

. . . .

*God, remind me to be a loyal friend and family member
in all my in-person conversations, all my online
interactions, and all the texts and emails I send.*

LABELS

*They surround me with hateful words and attack
me without cause. In return for my love they
accuse me, but I continue to pray.*
PSALM 109:3-4 HCSB

. . . .

Has anyone ever given you a label that you thought you'd never be able to escape? Maybe you're the crybaby in the family. Or maybe at school you're known as a klutz. Maybe you did something you regret, and now no one will let you live it down. Maybe you didn't even do the thing that people say you did, yet you still can't escape the label that goes along with that behavior.

God doesn't care about labels. Rahab in the Old Testament is a good example. Rahab was living a far from godly life. She probably got called some ugly names. Yet that's not why we remember her name today. Instead, she's remembered for her courage. God didn't look down on her because of the label she carried. Instead, He chose her to be one of Jesus' ancestors. He used her life in amazing ways.

No matter what labels you've been given—whether they're true or they're lies—God sees past them. He knows who you *really* are.

. . . .

*Thank You, God, that You see me and know me and love
me. Help me not to be defined by the labels my friends
and family have given me. May I rise past them
so that people see me for who I really am.*

REJECTION

*Even if my father and mother abandon me,
the LORD will hold me close.*
PSALM 27:10 NLT

All of us have to deal with rejection in our lives. We don't make the team; we don't get picked to be in the class play; boyfriends break up with us; friends decide they want to hang with another clique. Whatever form rejection takes, it always hurts. It makes us feel as though we're not as good as we'd hoped. And when the person who rejects us is someone close to us, it hurts even more.

Jesus understands rejection. The people from His hometown didn't believe He was who He claimed to be. Even some of His own family members rejected Him. One of His friends betrayed Him to the authorities who wanted to kill Him, and another friend refused to admit that he even knew Jesus.

No matter who rejects you, know that Jesus understands how you feel and He will never ever reject you!

Jesus, I'm so sorry that You were rejected by so many people during Your time on earth. I'm even sorrier for the times that I've rejected You. Thank You that when I feel as though everyone else has abandoned me, You are holding me close. You will never reject me.

ROMANCE

Daughters of Jerusalem, I charge you:
Do not arouse or awaken love until it so desires.
SONG OF SONGS 8:4 NIV

. . . .

The teen years are the time in our lives when romantic attractions can seem desperately important. Even a smile from that special someone has the power to make our day—and rejection from that person feels like it will destroy us.

These are normal feelings; but when it comes to romance, here are a few things to keep in mind:

- Depend on Jesus for your identity. Don't allow a romantic relationship to be your source of self-esteem.
- Make sure you're treated with respect in any relationship you enter. Don't think you can change someone into being a different sort of person.
- Look for someone who shares your interests and values. Don't use appearance as your main criterion.
- Stay true to yourself and to your relationship with God. Don't let anyone push you into doing things you're not comfortable doing.
- Don't be in a hurry. You have a whole lifetime to explore these feelings. Don't rush into an exclusive relationship with someone.

This is a special time of your life, filled with excitement and fun. God wants to bless *all* of your experiences, including your romances. Don't shut Him out of your love life!

. . . .

God, You know how much I long to have a special
relationship with someone. Help me to
wait for Your timing.

FAMILY

Exploit or abuse your family, and end up with a fistful of air; common sense tells you it's a stupid way to live.
PROVERBS 11:29 MSG

. . . .

Our families can be many good things. They can give us a sense of security and safety. We have fun with them, and we may love celebrating holidays and birthdays with these people who share our blood and our home. But no one ever said that living in a family is easy. Our families can drive us crazy. Their irritating habits get on our nerves. They can be bossy and annoying and impossible to live with.

But the Bible tells us we need our families. If we don't treat them right, ultimately, we hurt ourselves as much as we hurt them. When we push our families away, we may think we're grabbing our own rights and freedom. If we're not careful, though, we'll end up with nothing but a handful of air!

. . . .

God, show me tonight if I've been misusing my family members in any way. Have I been exploiting them or treating them without respect? When I feel impatient with my family, give me Your love and peace. Help me to show them Your love.

HUMILITY

*Always be humble and gentle. Be patient with each
other, making allowance for each other's
faults because of your love.*

EPHESIANS 4:2 NLT

. . . .

When our friends and family annoy us, the Bible asks that
we make allowances for one another. If your little brother
or sister is being particularly irritating, ask yourself if
there's something going on in your sibling's life. Is there
anything you might be able to do for your sibling? If one
of your parents snaps at you, think about how you want to
respond. What would happen if you asked, "Is everything
okay? Is there anything I can do to help?" Or if one of your
friends says something unkind to you, maybe you could
ask, "What's going on? Is something wrong?"

Remember, no one's perfect. You're not perfect either!
The more you can keep that in mind—in other words, the
humbler you are—the more you'll be able to be gentle and
patient with the people close to you.

. . . .

*God, when my friends and family bug me, remind me
that I'm also far from perfect. Help me be more
patient. Instead of getting angry at them,
show me how to help them.*

BOUND TOGETHER WITH PEACE

Make every effort to keep yourselves united in the Spirit,
binding yourselves together with peace.

EPHESIANS 4:3 NLT

· ·

The kind of peace that the Bible talks about isn't just the absence of conflict. The word used here in the Bible's original language means "all the pieces working together in harmony." It's a condition of health and wholeness that comes from the presence of God.

We see this peace in Jesus' life. It wasn't that He didn't have troubles—He did!—but He had something inside Him that was stronger and more real than anything that was happening in the outside world. That peace was what gave Him the power to calm a stormy sea. It was also what allowed Him to reach out and heal a soldier who threatened His life in the garden of Gethsemane.

When we give the peace of Jesus room in our lives, our relationships change. It's not always easy. It takes some effort on our part. But God's peace has the power to mend broken relationships and soothe hurt feelings. It draws our hearts together with the people we love. It unites us at a deeper level than anything we could manufacture in our own power.

· ·

Thank You, Jesus, for sharing Your peace with me.
Tomorrow, as I interact with my friends and family,
remind me to work hard to let Your
peace control every situation.

TRUE LOVE

Don't become partners with those who reject God.
How can you make a partnership out of right and wrong?
That's not partnership; that's war. Is light best friends
with dark? . . . Do trust and mistrust hold hands?
2 CORINTHIANS 6:14–15 MSG

. . . .

People *love* love. Not just teenagers either. Adults are also obsessed with love. TV shows, movies, and romance novels all describe love relationships, but those descriptions may not be very realistic. They can give us false expectations. We can end up hoping for something that no human being is capable of giving us.

Real love looks out for the interests of the other person, but it also insists on being treated with equal respect. Real love doesn't ask either person to compromise their values or beliefs. It doesn't try to persuade the other person to do things they don't want to do. That also means that you don't want to be romantically involved with someone who makes fun of people or someone who cares only about having fun, no matter who or what gets hurt.

True love is built on respect, shared interests and values, and mutual trust. And because it understands that no human can be *everything* for someone else, it relies on God to be the foundation of the relationship.

. . . .

God, be in all my relationships.
Teach me what true love is. May I always follow You.

PEER PRESSURE

But even if you suffer for doing what is right,
God will reward you for it. So don't worry
or be afraid of their threats.
1 PETER 3:14 NLT

Peer pressure, that feeling that you have to do something to be accepted, can be tough to handle. Usually, the pressure isn't as obvious as someone threatening to hurt you if you don't go along with the group; but even if it's unspoken, the threat of rejection is there.

If you've decided to follow God's plan for your life, you want to listen to His voice more than you want to listen to your friends'. But it's not easy. Here are some ideas to help you cope better with peer pressure:

- Give yourself permission to avoid situations where you may feel pressured to do something.
- If you're already in a situation like that, find a reason to leave.
- Choose to spend time with people who share your values—or at least respect your right to make your own choices.
- Ask for God's help ahead of time. You can also ask Him for help when you're in the middle of the situation—but don't wait until then!

Resisting peer pressure can make you feel embarrassed and uncomfortable, but God will reward you!

God, if I'm going to run into peer pressure tomorrow,
I'm asking You right now to make me wise
and strong enough to follow You.

JESUS NEVER CHANGES

*Jesus Christ is the same yesterday
and today and forever.*
HEBREWS 13:8 NASB

. . . .

Adolescence is a time of big changes. Your friends' appearances can sometimes seem to change overnight, with little girls suddenly getting curves and little boys sprouting beards. As you get older, you may see your parents and other adults in your life differently. Most of all, *you* keep changing. The things you like doing are different from what you used to enjoy a few years ago. You have new interests, new feelings, and new ideas. With so much changing so quickly, life can seem scary sometimes. What is there to hold on to when nothing stays the same?

No matter how much we, our family, and our friends change, Jesus never changes. He remains the same. He stays with us through all the changes. He keeps us secure. He's the unshifting foundation that lies beneath every other person and relationship in your life.

. . . .

*Jesus, when I feel unsettled and unsure because of all
the changes in the people I know, thank You that You
are always the same. Your love will keep me safe.*

ENCOURAGEMENT

*We must also consider how to encourage each other
to show love and to do good things.*
HEBREWS 10:24 GW

. . . .

God wants us to encourage the people around us. He wants us to help them to know Him better. Together, we show each other how to be the people God is calling us to be.

This doesn't mean we have to sit down and have prayer meetings with our friends and family (unless we want to!). Encouragement can be as fast and simple as sending a text saying "I'm praying for you" to your sister when you know she has a big test. It might mean you post an encouraging meme on a friend's Facebook page. It could even be something as small as giving your parents a smile to brighten their day. All those things each take about ten seconds to do—so no matter how busy we are, we can find time for encouragement.

Think about what you could do right now or during the day tomorrow. Your small message of encouragement could have a lasting impact on someone's day. Maybe even on their whole life.

. . . .

*God, show me how I can encourage the people
in my life. I want them to be the best they
can be. I want to show them Your love.*

LET'S GET TOGETHER!

*We should not stop gathering together with other
believers, as some of you are doing. Instead,
we must continue to encourage each other.*
HEBREWS 10:25 GW

. . . .

Today's technology allows us to be more connected with other people than ever before. At the same time, it can get in the way of *real* connection. Texts, email, and social-media apps can all be used to serve God. But sometimes, when we're connected thumb to thumb instead of face to face, we can lose the soul connections we need. It's easier to be fake when we're not talking to someone in person. Because we don't have the clues that body language and facial expressions give us, we may not notice when our friends need extra encouragement from us.

So, don't stop getting together with others, especially the people who encourage you to get to know God better. Even though we need our alone time with God, we also need to learn from one another.

. . . .

*God, thank You for the people You've put in my life.
I want to bless them, and I want to allow them to bless me.
Be present in my friendships, and help us to encourage
one another to be all that You want us to be.*

BLESS!

Summing up: Be agreeable, be sympathetic, be loving, be compassionate, be humble. That goes for all of you, no exceptions. No retaliation. No sharp-tongued sarcasm. Instead, bless—that's your job, to bless.
1 PETER 3:8–9 MSG

When it comes to your relationship with friends and family, the Bible is full of sound, practical advice. It can teach you how to get along better with others. It all comes down to a few simple things: Show sympathy to one another. Express your love for each other in action. Don't be conceited or put yourself first; have humility. Don't get even. Don't be sarcastic or make fun of others.

Bottom line? Bless others. That's your job.

But what, exactly, does it mean to bless other people? The word that the Bible uses here has to do with giving gifts. That doesn't mean we have to wrap up presents for all our friends and family (although there's nothing wrong with that). Gifts come in many shapes and sizes. A gift could be a helping hand, a listening ear, a sympathetic smile, or an understanding heart. When we bless others, we give something of ourselves to them. We want only good things for them, and we allow God's blessings to flow through us.

God, show me how to bless the people in my life. As I fall asleep tonight, bring to my mind a few specific things I could do tomorrow that would bless my friends and family.

Your Words and Actions

SEXUAL URGES

Stay away from lusts which tempt young people.
Pursue what has God's approval.
Pursue faith, love, and peace.
2 Timothy 2:22 GW

. . . .

During adolescence, people are especially aware of what's going on with their bodies and everybody else's. That's a fact that hasn't changed for thousands of years. It's why the Bible warns about the lusts that tempt young people. The word used here in the Bible's original language means simply "urges" or "longings." There's nothing wrong with having those urges and longings. They're completely normal and healthy. But following those urges can lead you to actions that aren't what God wants for your life.

It makes sense to stay away from situations that make those urges particularly strong. It may even mean that you limit how much time you spend alone with your significant other (because face it, you're a lot less likely to yield to temptation if you're with a group of people than if the two of you are all alone somewhere private).

You're going to think about sex. You're a teenager! But focus more on faith, love, and peace—and ask God to help you handle your urges.

. . . .

God, may all my actions please You.
Keep my life on track.

SPEAKING THE TRUTH WITH LOVE

As we lovingly speak the truth, we will grow up completely in our relationship to Christ.
EPHESIANS 4:15 GW

. . . .

Do you speak the truth or do you lie just a little? Maybe you exaggerate a little when you're telling your friends about something that happened to you, just to make the story more interesting. Or maybe you stretch the truth with your parents so you won't get in trouble. You may not tell *big* lies, but the Bible says even little lies matter.

You're not alone if you've gotten into the habit of lying. A lot of people do. We tell ourselves our lies don't hurt anyone. But if we step back and take an honest look at ourselves (and sometimes, it's hard to be honest even with ourselves), we may find that our dishonesty isn't as harmless as we want to think.

Ask yourself, *What motivates my lies?* Do you want to make yourself look better to your friends? Do you want to give yourself more control over your life by hiding what you're doing? What are you covering up? In most cases, we lie for two reasons: because we're insecure or because we're selfish.

The Bible says that when we truly love and know that we're loved, we're not afraid. We stop putting ourselves first. We trust God to take care of us. We don't have to lie anymore.

. . . .

God, show me if I've been dishonest.
Help me to love You enough to tell the truth.

YOUR GOD-FASHIONED PHONE

*Take on an entirely new way of life—a God-fashioned life,
a life renewed from the inside and working itself
into your conduct as God accurately
reproduces his character in you.*

EPHESIANS 4:24 MSG

Our phones are a huge part of our lives today. God's big enough to include our phones in His plan for our lives. He's not going to ask you to give up your phone and go back to living like your parents did before the invention of cell phones. But He does want you to use your phone to serve Him. This means that you're careful what you text. You make sure that every word you put online is kind, encouraging, and loving.

Your phone can also be a tool that encourages you to live more closely to God. For example, you could set your phone's alarm to go off with a reminder at certain times during the day: *Stop and pray!* Even a few seconds of prayer (a simple "Hello, God" or "Help me!") can make a huge difference in your day. Or the reminder might be *Say something kind to someone* or *Tell God thank You for something* or *Pray for Mom while she's at work.* You might also use a Bible app on your phone. You can read the Bible on your phone or have a Bible verse sent to you every morning. Your phone can be part of your new God-fashioned life.

*God, make my phone Your tool
for bringing me closer to You.*

A ROOTED LIFE

Just as you accepted Christ Jesus as your Lord, you must
continue to follow him. Let your roots grow down
into him, and let your lives be built on him.
COLOSSIANS 2:6–7 NLT

. . . .

You may hear a lot at church about accepting Jesus as
your personal Savior. Deciding to let Jesus into your life
is an important step to take, but God doesn't want you to
stop there. He wants you to keep on following Jesus in
big ways and small. He wants everything you do and say
to be shaped by Jesus.

This won't happen automatically. You'll need to spend
daily time talking to Jesus and learning more about Him.
But you know how old married couples start to look, talk,
and act like each other? The same sort of thing will happen
with you and Jesus. The more time you spend together,
the more you'll become like Him. Your life will be rooted
in Him. Your entire life will be built on Him.

. . . .

Jesus, I want to keep following You. Show me now,
in this time we have together, how to do that.
Be the foundation of my life. Be the roots
that give me life. Make me act like You.

TAKE UP YOUR CROSS

"If any of you wants to be my follower, you must give up your own way, take up your cross, and follow me."

MARK 8:34 NLT

. . . .

What does it mean to "take up your cross"? It means that Jesus is calling us to put others ahead of ourselves. And that's hard. Our world teaches us to put ourselves first. It's going against the grain to say no to our selfish urges and desires.

Notice that this verse says to take up *your* cross. Jesus is saying here that your cross will be your own. It will be different from everyone else's. What comes easy to one person may be hard for you to do. What is easy for you might be difficult for someone else. There's no room for pride here. We all must shoulder our own cross. We have to say no to our selfishness no matter what form it takes, and we have to say yes to Jesus. We have to say yes to doing whatever we can for others. But when we say, "Jesus, I give up my selfish desires for the good of the people around me," we find that God provides for us in ways we never dreamed could be possible.

. . . .

Jesus, it's so hard to say no to my selfishness. But I know that You were willing to carry an actual cross because You loved me. Give me the strength tomorrow to carry my own cross for You and for those around me.

NO MORE LIES!

Do not lie to each other, since you have taken off your old self with its practices and have put on the new self, which is being renewed in knowledge in the image of its Creator.
COLOSSIANS 3:9-10 NIV

. . . .

The Bible makes a big deal about lies, and yet our world says it's okay to lie. A recent study found that 91 percent of people say they lie regularly. The main reason given for all that lying is to "save face" and to "not offend people." Another survey, this one done with only teenagers, found that 92 percent of the young people admitted to lying to their parents at least once in the previous year, and 73 percent said they lied at least once a week.

So, what's the take-away here? Should we say to ourselves, *Well, since everyone is doing it, my lies aren't so bad?* No, that's *not* what God wants! God wants you to be a new person, different from the one you used to be. He wants our communications with others to be trustworthy. He knows that distrust separates people. Honesty is the foundation for communication between people. It promotes understanding. It puts others' needs ahead of our own. When we're honest, we want what's best for the other person even if it makes us look bad.

. . . .

God, tonight, as I look at myself and my life, show me any dishonesty I've been holding on to. Make me into a new person—a person who doesn't tell lies.

GOALS

I can't consider myself a winner yet. This is what I do: I don't look back, I lengthen my stride, and I run straight toward the goal to win the prize that God's heavenly call offers in Christ Jesus. Whoever has a mature faith should think this way. And if you think differently, God will show you how to think.

PHILIPPIANS 3:13–15 GW

Goals give us something to work toward. They give our lives direction. They help motivate us to change our old habits. They keep us from focusing on the past and being discouraged by old failures.

The Bible says that our biggest goal should be to become like Jesus. That should be our number-one priority. So here are actions we can take that will get us closer to that goal:

- Pray. Without regular time with God, we'll lose sight of the goal.
- Read the Bible. We can find who Jesus really is by reading about Him.
- Get together with other people to encourage each other, learn about God together, and worship Him.

Jesus, I have a lot of little goals for my life, but becoming like You is my biggest goal. Show me tonight, tomorrow, and each and every day what I need to do to keep running straight toward You.

THE ANIMALS IN YOUR LIFE

Good people are good to their animals.
PROVERBS 12:10 MSG

· ·

God blesses you—He gives Himself to you—through each detail of your life. That includes your pets. Animals are good at showing us unconditional love. They don't judge us. They don't care if our hair is dirty or if we've gained five pounds. In their eyes, we're always perfect. And in that sense, they show us God and His love.

By the same token, one of the ways we can serve God is by taking good care of the animals in our lives. The Bible tells us that God cares about the sparrows (Matthew 10:29), so it's a pretty safe bet He also cares for your dog or cat or even your goldfish or hamster. After all, He made all creation, including animals, and ultimately they belong to Him. The Bible says, "For every animal of the forest is mine, and the cattle on a thousand hills" (Psalm 50:10 NIV). When you are responsible about taking care of these small helpless creatures in your care, God is pleased.

· ·

*Thank You, God, for the animals You've put in my life.
I'm grateful for the ways they teach me to know You better.
And in the same way that You never forget to take good
care of me, may I always take good care of them.*

YOU'RE NEVER TOO BUSY FOR GOD

*"First, be concerned about his kingdom
and what has his approval."*
MATTHEW 6:33 GW

. . . .

Have you noticed that the older you get, the busier you are? It's hard to find time for everything, even the things you really want to do. The things that keep you busy are often good things too—such as participating in sports or music, helping your family, working at a job, or spending time with your friends. And then there's your schoolwork, not to mention church and any volunteer activities you're involved in.

God blesses you through all these things. They are His gifts to you. But He also wants you to live your life in such a way that you always put Him first. Don't get so busy with all the many good things in your life that you forget about the one best thing—Jesus. Make following Him your number-one priority.

. . . .

*Jesus, thank You for all the ways You use my life to bless
me. Remind me, though, to never get so busy that
I forget You. May everything I do serve
You. Be at the center of my life.*

CARING FOR GOD'S EARTH

"This is what I will do if you will live by my laws and carefully obey my commands: I will give you rain at the right time. The land will produce its crops, and the trees in the field will produce their fruit."

LEVITICUS 26:3–4 GW

· ·

The way we live not only affects other people; it affects the planet that God has given us as our home. Human greed and selfishness take their toll on the earth. We are so used to our conveniences that we consider them to be necessities; meanwhile, pollution from our cars and factories and homes is a growing problem.

The answers aren't simple. We need to carefully examine our lives. When God has first place, we'll live in harmony not only with other human beings but also with the natural world. We'll live in the way God always intended us to live, blessing the earth while it blesses us in return.

· ·

In my time alone with You, God, point out anything in me that's out of place. Show me the areas where my selfishness is ruling my life instead of You ruling it. Please use me to bless Your creation and not destroy it. May my words and actions also inspire others to take responsibility for Your world more seriously.

OPEN ARMS

She opens her arms to the poor and
extends her hands to the needy.
PROVERBS 31:20 NIV

. . . .

If you want to learn about God's idea of what it means to
be a woman, read Proverbs 31. This portion of scripture
paints a picture of a strong, intelligent, competent, and
creative woman. She's busy with many things, including
helping those who are less fortunate than she is.

Make this woman your role model. Try to live her life
as she did. When you do, that will include reaching out
your hands to help the poor. This could mean volunteering
in a soup kitchen, donating your unneeded clothes and
household items to those who can use them, or giving your
money to support charities that help those in need. But
the poor aren't necessarily people who don't have enough
money. The poor can also be the kids at school who don't
have the same resources you do in terms of people to care
for them and support them. It might be someone no one
understands or likes. Sometimes people can have plenty
of money and still be poor. Ask God how He wants you to
open your arms to those in need.

. . . .

As I grow closer to You in this time we have together,
God, point out to me ways I can give to others.

PRISONERS

*Continue to remember those in prison as if you were
together with them in prison, and those who are
mistreated as if you yourselves were suffering.*

HEBREWS 13:3 NIV

. . . .

We often think of people in prison as bad people. We don't
really want to have anything to do with people like them.
We assume that because of whatever crime they committed, they deserve to be where they are. And that may be
true. But God still wants us to remember that these men
and women are human beings. Instead of seeing them as
different and distant from us, He wants us to identify with
their loneliness and suffering. After all, we may not have
committed any crimes, but we too have sinned.

There are also different kinds of prisons. Addiction
to drugs or alcohol can be a sort of prison, for example.
A physical or mental disability could be another form of
prison. Ask God to show you how you can demonstrate
His love to people who are locked up in any way.

. . . .

*God, tonight I am praying for anyone who is in prison
because of a crime they committed. I pray for those who
have been imprisoned unjustly. And I pray for people
who are trapped by the circumstances of their lives.
May I never forget these people. Remind me to
carry them in my heart, just as You do.*

FOREIGNERS, ORPHANS, AND WIDOWS

"Give. . .to the foreigners living among you, the orphans,
and the widows in your towns, so they can eat
and be satisfied. Then the LORD your God
will bless you in all your work."
DEUTERONOMY 14:29 NLT

God cares about anyone who is lonely and rejected, anyone who is struggling to be accepted. That includes those who have lost their parents or their spouses, as well as those who are strangers, people who are new to your school or town. Again and again throughout the Bible, God's Word makes clear that He expects us to help people like this.

They may need our practical help. An older woman living alone, for instance, might need your help shoveling her driveway or buying groceries. Children without parents could benefit from an older teen spending time with them and giving them attention. People who are new to the area would appreciate being welcomed to the neighborhood with cookies or a flowering plant.

We should also remember to reach out in genuine friendship to all these people. More than anything else, they may need someone who's willing to give them a friendly smile and listen to them when they talk, someone who won't judge them for being different. Someone who will carry the love of Christ to them!

*Jesus, I want to carry Your love to the world.
Give me opportunities to help those who are lonely.*

FEEDING YOUR ENEMIES

If your enemies are hungry, give them food to eat.
If they are thirsty, give them water to drink.
PROVERBS 25:21 NLT

. . . .

We don't usually invite our enemies to come over to our house for dinner. We generally take for granted that we want to avoid those people. After all, there's a reason they're our enemies. These are people we believe want to hurt us in some way or another. They're not like us. They don't believe the same things we do about God or about how to live life. So why would God want us to share a meal with them?

But that is exactly what God wants us to do. He wants us to treat our enemies the same way we treat our friends—with thoughtfulness and consideration. This may mean that we literally give them food or a drink. It could also mean that we notice when they're lonely or sad, and we reach out to them with kindness and compassion. Most of all, it will mean that we bring to them the Bread of Life and the Living Water that is Jesus.

. . . .

Jesus, I know You are the food and drink that all our souls need. May I carry You to everyone, even the people I consider to be enemies.

DEFENDING THE WEAK

"Defend the weak, the poor, and the fatherless. Maintain the rights of the poor and oppressed."
PSALM 82:3 WEB

. . . .

Following Jesus means that you serve Him with your body, your mind, your emotions, your soul, and your relationships. Sometimes we focus so much on all those aspects of our lives with Jesus that we forget that He also wants us to be busy caring for those who are poor, weak, or in trouble. The Bible makes this very clear, though. In fact, all through its pages it tells us over and over that God's followers help others.

Don't assume that because you're a teenager there's nothing you can do to stand up for those who are in trouble. Look around your school. If you pay attention, you'll start to notice the kids who are overlooked and rejected. They may be the kids who dress differently or smell a little funny, the kids others make fun of, or the ones who don't have any friends. Take a stand for those kids. Be their friend. Defend them.

. . . .

Jesus, I feel a little scared and embarrassed when I think about standing up for the kids no one likes. Give me courage to act the way You would. I know You never rejected anyone. Remind me how important this is to You.

LOVE YOUR ENEMIES

"I'm telling you to love your enemies. Let them bring out the best in you, not the worst. When someone gives you a hard time, respond with the energies of prayer, for then you are working out of your true selves, your God-created selves. This is what God does. He gives his best—the sun to warm and the rain to nourish—to everyone, regardless: the good and bad, the nice and nasty. If all you do is love the lovable, do you expect a bonus? Anybody can do that. If you simply say hello to those who greet you, do you expect a medal? Any run-of-the-mill sinner does that."
MATTHEW 5:44–47 MSG

. . . .

Being kind to our enemies is one thing. But *loving* them? That seems like God's asking too much! And yet that is exactly what Jesus is telling us to do in these verses.

Notice something else that He's saying here. Not only are we to love our enemies for their sakes, but we're also to do it for our own good. God can use our enemies to bring out the best in us. They can help us become our true selves, the people God created us to be.

God loves everyone the same. The worst criminal is as precious to Him as the most innocent, beautiful baby. And now He wants us to learn to be like Him.

. . . .

Help me, Jesus, to act in love toward the people who are mean to me, the people I have a hard time liking let alone loving. Change me, day by day, until I become more like You.

WHAT'S IMPORTANT TO YOU?

A man came up to Jesus and asked, "Teacher, what good thing must I do to get eternal life?" "Why do you ask me about what is good?" Jesus replied. "There is only One who is good. If you want to enter life, keep the commandments." "Which ones?" he inquired. Jesus replied, " 'You shall not murder, you shall not commit adultery, you shall not steal, you shall not give false testimony, honor your father and mother,' and 'love your neighbor as yourself.' " "All these I have kept," the young man said. "What do I still lack?" Jesus answered, "If you want to be perfect, go, sell your possessions and give to the poor, and you will have treasure in heaven. Then come, follow me." When the young man heard this, he went away sad, because he had great wealth.

MATTHEW 19:16–22 NIV

. . . .

The young man in this story wanted to *do* something in order to live with Jesus in eternity. What Jesus says to him doesn't mean that we all must give away everything we own and become homeless people. What it means is that *nothing* in our lives should be as important to us as Jesus. He is the only One who can make us good.

. . . .

Jesus, show me tonight if there's something in my life that I've put ahead of You. And then give me the courage to give it back to You. I want You to be first.

SHARING

Be generous and willing to share.
1 TIMOTHY 6:18 NIV

When you were a little kid, you probably got reminded fairly often to share. It's an action that just doesn't come naturally to most human beings. From the time we're able to talk, we've wanted to say, "Mine!" As we get older, we may learn to fake it better. We know it doesn't look so cool if we hog all the cake or refuse to take turns playing a video game. But even adults have a hard time sharing.

God has given us so much. Our lives are filled with blessings that include all sorts of things—a house to live in and food to eat, intellectual abilities and creative talents, physical strengths, friendships, and family. And God wants us to be willing to share it *all*, holding nothing back. He wants us to stop saying, "Mine!" and instead say to Him, "Yours. Use this thing that You've given me however You want. I'm giving it back to You. Show me how to share it with others."

God, thank You that You've shared everything with me—life, love, and countless blessings. You've made me rich in so many ways. Tonight, as we spend time together, remind me of ways I can share with others the many blessings that You've given me.

HOW TO CONTROL YOUR TONGUE

*If you claim to be religious but don't control your tongue,
you are fooling yourself, and your religion is worthless.*
JAMES 1:26 NLT

. . . .

There's a saying that's a good reminder for us all: "Before you open your mouth to speak, always ask yourself two questions: *Is it true?* and *Is it constructive?*" (In other words, will it build up or strengthen others? Or will it tear them down, making it harder for them to see what God is doing in their lives?) Asking yourself those two questions *every* time you speak seems like a lot of work, doesn't it? But we can at least keep these questions at the back of our minds throughout the day as we interact with other people. We can't claim to be following Jesus if we make a habit of lying, gossiping, and using words that are ugly and hurtful.

Speech is one of God's greatest gifts to human beings. Imagine what it would be like if we couldn't talk to each other! But like all of God's gifts, He wants us to use it with care, in a way that honors Him.

. . . .

*God, when I'm with my friends, it's so easy to just open my
mouth and let words pour out. Before I know it, I've said
something hurtful. Or I start to gossip. Or I tell a lie.
Please forgive me. Tomorrow, remind me before I get
carried away to ask myself, Is it true? Is it constructive?*

GOD'S BODY ON EARTH

Give your bodies to God. . .Let them be a living
and holy sacrifice—the kind he will find acceptable.
This is truly the way to worship him.
ROMANS 12:1 NLT

. . . .

Back in the sixteenth century, a woman named Teresa of Avila wrote these words: "Christ has no body now on earth but yours, no hands but yours, no feet but yours; Yours are the eyes through which to look out Christ's compassion to the world; Yours are the feet with which He is to go about doing good; Yours are the hands with which He is to bless men now."

That's what it means to be a "living sacrifice." We don't have to die for Jesus. We have to *live* for Jesus. We give Him the freedom to use our hands, our feet, our eyes, and our mouths as expressions of His love. Here are just a few specific ways that might work:

- Help your brother, sister, or friend study for a test.
- Help an elderly neighbor by doing yard work.
- Use your talents—whatever they are—to worship God publicly at church.
- Speak up when kids are being mean to someone.
- Get involved with your community to make it a safer, more beautiful place.
- Volunteer at your local hospital or nursing home.

. . . .

God, tonight, as I settle down for sleep,
give me some ideas about how You can use me
tomorrow. I can't wait to get started!

WORDS AGAIN!

Though some tongues just love the taste of gossip, those who follow Jesus have better uses for language than that. Don't talk dirty or silly. That kind of talk doesn't fit our style. Thanksgiving is our dialect.

EPHESIANS 5:4 MSG

. . . .

The Bible talks *a lot* about the words that come out of our mouths. These days, though, our words don't only come out of our mouths. They also come out of our fingers onto our phones and computer screens. And the bad thing about those words is that they don't go away. They're a written record.

You probably have a pretty good idea what this verse means when it says, "Don't talk dirty or silly." Here are some other don'ts that go along with that, whether you're using your fingers or your mouth to talk:

- Don't tell secrets.
- Don't spread rumors.
- Don't insult others.
- Don't encourage others to be unkind.

Make thanksgiving your "dialect." In other words, use your words to thank God for everything He has given you.

. . . .

God, thank You. Thank You, thank You, thank You. I know I don't say it enough. Fill my mind with all You've done for me so that when I talk or text, I never forget to honor You.

JESUS IS EVERYWHERE IN EVERYONE

*" 'I was hungry and you gave me something to eat,
I was thirsty and you gave me something to drink, I was a
stranger and you invited me in, I needed clothes and you
clothed me, I was sick and you looked after me, I was in
prison and you came to visit me.' Then the righteous will
answer him, 'Lord, when did we see you hungry and feed
you, or thirsty and give you something to drink? When did
we see you a stranger and invite you in, or needing clothes
and clothe you? When did we see you sick or in prison
and go to visit you?' The King will reply, 'Truly I tell
you, whatever you did for one of the least of these
brothers and sisters of mine, you did for me.' "*
MATTHEW 25:35–40 NIV

. . . .

Jesus told this story to remind us that He is present in
unexpected places. He doesn't just hang out in church.

Tomorrow, take a good look around you, and then
remind yourself, *That kid who no one likes—that's Jesus. The
mean teacher everyone hates—that's Jesus. The new kid who
dresses funny—that's Jesus. The crabby old lady across the
street—she's Jesus. The tired-looking man at the checkout
counter—he's Jesus too.* When you see Jesus everywhere,
how will that change how you act?

. . . .

*Jesus, remind me that You are truly present in every
person I'll run into tomorrow. May I treat each
and every one the way I'd treat You.*

STRANGERS

Love ye therefore the stranger:
for ye were strangers in the land of Egypt.
Deuteronomy 10:19 KJV

. . . .

Human beings have a hard time with people who seem strange and different. It just seems to be part of our make-up to feel uncomfortable with newcomers, people who don't fit in with "us." We think they could be a threat to us in some way. They scare us or make us uneasy, so we pull away from them.

Strangers come in many forms. Maybe they wear different clothes than we do. They might speak a different language. They could worship God differently than we do. But they don't necessarily have to come from another country to be a "stranger." A stranger is anyone who doesn't fit in—the nerdy kid, the kid whose clothes are out of style, the kid who smells a little odd, the kid who talks with a funny accent.

God asks us to put ourselves in the stranger's place. We've all been in situations where we felt as though we didn't belong. We need to remember what that feels like and then reach out in love to everyone around us, no matter who they are, what they look like, or how they talk.

. . . .

God, I know You don't want me to feel scared
or uncomfortable around people who seem
strange to me. Teach me to see You in these
individuals. Remind me to be kind.

WORDS THAT HURT

Don't say anything that would hurt another person.
Instead, speak only what is good so that you can give
help wherever it is needed. That way, what you
say will help those who hear you.
EPHESIANS 4:29 GW

. . . .

According to some studies, the average person speaks between 10,000 and 25,000 words a day. That's a whole lot of words to keep track of!

Words can hurt other people. They also have the power to hurt us. If you say things such as "I'm so dumb" or "I look so ugly today," you're giving yourself messages that go against what God says about you. And if you're constantly complaining about your life, that will also shape the direction your life goes. The more you say your life is awful, the more awful it will feel.

If you find yourself feeling depressed or discouraged, pay attention to the words you've been using. You don't need to go around telling people how smart and pretty you are, but you shouldn't be running yourself down either. Words set the tone for your life. They'll shape the kind of day you'll have tomorrow.

. . . .

Tomorrow, God, remind me again and again to use my
words for You. Teach me to be more positive, to say things
that will make me and others feel happier, not sadder or
angrier. Help me to use my words the way You want.

ONLINE WORDS

Now is the time to get rid of anger, rage,
malicious behavior, slander, and dirty language.
COLOSSIANS 3:8 NLT

. . . .

Here it is *again!* Once more the Bible is telling us to be careful with our words. Facebook (or whatever social-media app you use) is one of the places where we need to be particularly careful.

Let's say a friend of yours posts a photo of herself that's not very becoming. You comment, "Ew!" You truly don't mean to be unkind to your friend. You're just saying that the picture doesn't do her justice. But then someone else makes a longer comment that's triggered by your one tiny comment. More and more people get involved. An argument explodes with people making accusations. When you see your friend at school, she turns away and won't speak to you all because of a silly misunderstanding on Facebook.

Whenever we're online, we need to be even more careful of our words than we are in person. It's too easy to be misunderstood. Here are a few helpful guidelines:

- Don't post *anything* that's negative.
- Don't return evil for evil. In other words, if someone posts something that sounds negative, don't respond with negative comments of your own.
- Be kind. Even when it hurts.

. . . .

Jesus, may ALL my words honor You.
Remind me to be particularly careful when I'm online.

WORK

Always work enthusiastically for the Lord, for you know that nothing you do for the Lord is ever useless.
1 CORINTHIANS 15:58 NLT

. . . .

Have you ever heard the saying "God helps those who help themselves"? There's some truth to it. If you need an extra hundred dollars to pay for a prom dress, God probably won't miraculously drop the money in your lap, but He might give you the opportunity to earn it (though even then, you'll probably have to put some effort into looking for work that pays). And God probably won't help you pass a big exam if you never prepared for it ahead of time. Hopefully, that's just common sense. But we don't have to work to *earn* God's love and help. It's free for the asking.

Instead, whatever we're doing, God wants us to do it for Him. If you're working to earn some extra money, do that work for God. If you're studying for a test, give that work to God too. When you think of your work in this way, you give God room to act alongside you. Things may not turn out exactly the way you want, but nothing you do for God is ever useless.

. . . .

*Remind me to do everything tomorrow for You, God.
Take my work—at home, at school, everywhere—
and use it to bless others and myself.
May my work always honor You.*

LOVE IN ACTION

*If I give everything I own to the poor and even go to the
stake to be burned as a martyr, but I don't love, I've gotten
nowhere. So, no matter what I say, what I believe,
and what I do, I'm bankrupt without love.*

1 CORINTHIANS 13:3 MSG

God wants us to actively serve Him. We do that by reaching
out to others in all sorts of practical down-to-earth ways.
But this verse is saying that we need the right motivation
behind our actions. If we do volunteer work just to impress
other people, it doesn't matter how many hours we devote
to helping others. Without love, our work is empty and
meaningless. It doesn't matter how many Bible verses
we can quote or how good we are at talking about faith
and being a Christian. Without love, those things don't
matter either.

As we express love in action, we too will be changed.
It's a two-way street. We'll find we can see past our own
self-centeredness more easily. We'll experience more
happiness and peace in our lives.

Love must be expressed in words and actions. They go
together. Love that's not backed up by action isn't truly
love. And actions and words without love don't amount
to much.

*God, make me rich with love so that love
spills out of me in action and word.*

SMALL THINGS WITH GREAT LOVE

Each one of us needs to look after the good of the people around us, asking ourselves, "How can I help?"
ROMANS 15:2 MSG

. . . .

Here's another one of the Bible's short, practical words of advice. It's really very simple. In every situation you encounter and in every relationship, ask yourself: *How can I help? How can I make things better in these circumstances? How can I make this person feel better about himself? How can I brighten that person's day?* It doesn't matter how tiny your efforts are. Sometimes even a smile can make all the difference. There's a saying (often attributed to Mother Teresa) that goes like this: "Not all of us can do great things. But we can do small things with great love."

Love in action can be expressed by our facial expressions and the way we look at each other. It can go out into the world through the work we do and the words we speak. This active love is what makes our world a better place. It makes us better people too. As we do whatever we can to help others, we'll find we can see past our own self-centeredness more easily. We'll learn to pay better attention to what other people need. We may find we have more in common with people who seem very different from ourselves than we first thought. Love changes things.

. . . .

God, change me with Your love, and then use me to carry Your love into the world. Show me where I can be of help to someone tomorrow.

ALCOHOL AND YOU

Don't drink too much wine. That cheapens your life.
Drink the Spirit of God, huge draughts of him.
EPHESIANS 5:18 MSG

. . . .

The Bible says that wine "gladdens" the human heart (Psalm 104:15 NIV). Jesus' first miracle was to turn water into wine at a wedding reception. (You can read about it in John 2.) But like all of God's gifts to us, there's a time and a place that's right for it—and times and places that aren't.

As a teenager, not only is alcohol against the law, but it also can harm your body and mind. Drink too much and you'll likely end up doing things you never would do otherwise. You could get in a fight with a friend, for example. Being drunk can even make you feel like you don't care about anything—leading to extremely poor choices. And we all know what can happen if you drink and drive.

God's not saying He doesn't want you to have any fun. He's saying that instead of using alcohol to give you confidence or happiness, drink His Spirit. Treasure and protect the gifts He's given you by not wasting them. Rely on the Spirit of God.

. . . .

God, I want to follow You in all things.
Help me to keep my eyes on You,
no matter what the people
around me are doing.

DON'T GET EVEN

"Here's what I propose: 'Don't hit back at all.' If someone strikes you, stand there and take it. If someone drags you into court and sues for the shirt off your back, giftwrap your best coat and make a present of it. And if someone takes unfair advantage of you, use the occasion to practice the servant life. No more tit-for-tat stuff. Live generously."
MATTHEW 5:39–42 MSG

. . . .

Sure, we know we're supposed to be kind and share with others. But if someone hurts us, are we supposed to not protect ourselves? If someone abuses us, are we supposed to just lie down and take it?

No. That's not what this verse is saying. God doesn't want you to be hurt. When Jesus was alive on earth, He made pretty clear that He respected and loved women, and He blessed the women who stood up for their rights.

What this scripture *is* saying is this: When someone hurts you, don't try to get even. If someone starts a fight with you, be kind to that person. If someone "borrows" something of yours and fails to return it, figure that she needs it more than you do. Be generous with your possessions. Be even more generous with forgiveness.

. . . .

Jesus, thank You that You forgave us when we rejected You. You showed us a new way to live—a way of love and forgiveness.

WITNESS

"But you will receive power when the Holy Spirit comes upon you. And you will be my witnesses, telling people about me everywhere."

ACTS 1:8 NLT

. . . .

How do you feel about public speaking? If you're like a lot of people, it's one of your least favorite things. The thought of standing up in front of people and giving a speech makes your stomach do flip-flops. So, when you read in the Bible that you're supposed to tell others about Jesus, it may make you feel pretty uncomfortable.

But there are a few things you should keep in mind. First, God wants you to share your faith naturally and respectfully; He doesn't want you to shove Him down people's throats or get in arguments. Second, the Holy Spirit will show you what to say and when to say it. Rely on the Spirit for direction.

Churches have often turned "witnessing" into something artificial and uncomfortable. The word *witness*, though, just means to tell what you know, the same way you'd tell someone about a book you read or a movie you saw. If you're excited about God, you'll want to talk about Him. It's that simple.

. . . .

Spirit, show me tomorrow how to talk about You. May my entire life—my words, my actions, and my attitudes—show You to others.

AGE DOESN'T MATTER!

Don't let anyone look down on you for being young.
Instead, make your speech, behavior, love, faith,
and purity an example for other believers.
1 TIMOTHY 4:12 GW

Do you ever feel like people look down on you because of your age? The adults in your life don't seem to take your ideas seriously. Maybe when you speak up about something, they disregard what you have to say.

The Bible says it doesn't matter how old you are. God doesn't care if you're six, sixteen, or sixty. In His eyes, you're valuable, no matter what your age is. He takes you seriously. And you don't have to wait to serve Him. Your life can be an example to others, whether they're younger than you, the same age as you, or older than you. God uses adults, He uses very old people, He uses little kids—and He wants to use you. You don't have to wait until you're older to get started. You can start changing your world right now.

Use me, God, in whatever way You want. May I serve
You in each thing I do tomorrow. May everyone—
including the adults in my life—see You in me.

DAILY BOOKENDS

It is good to give thanks to the LORD, to sing praises to the Most High. It is good to proclaim your unfailing love in the morning, your faithfulness in the evening.

PSALM 92:1–2 NLT

. . . .

Take a look at these verses, word by word:

1. The word *good*—the Hebrew word used here in the original version means simply "agreeable, pleasant, enjoyable."
2. *Thanks* seems pretty obvious, but the word in the original language also has to do with throwing something down. You say "Thank You" to God, and at the same time you give whatever it is back to Him.
3. The word translated as LORD is "Yahweh"—the Living One, the One who gives life.
4. *Sing praises* means exactly what it sounds like—make music that expresses our feelings for God.
5. *Most High* is a name for God that means He's more important, more loving, more kind, and better than anything else in life.
6. *Proclaim* here means "to make something conspicuous." We can use our words to proclaim God's love, but sometimes actions speak louder than words.
7. And finally, God's *unfailing love* and *faithfulness* in the morning and the evening mean that God is like a set of bookends that encloses our days. His love is reliable and firm. We can count on it throughout the entire day.

. . . .

God, may I use these words to guide me through the day tomorrow—and every day.